Giggle Time – Establishing the Social Connection

of related interest

Playing, Laughing and Learning with Children on the Autism Spectrum
A Practical Resource of Play Ideas for Parents and Carers
Julia Moor
ISBN 1 84310 060 6

My Social Story Book
Carol Gray
ISBN 1 85302 950 5

Relationship Development Intervention with Young Children
Social and Emotional Development Activities for Asperger Syndrome,
Autism, PDD and NLD
Steven E. Gutstein and Rachelle K. Sheely
ISBN 1 84310 714 7

Relationship Development Intervention with Children,
Adolescents and Adults
Social and Emotional Development Activities for Asperger Syndrome,
Autism, PDD and NLD
Steven E. Gutstein and Rachelle K. Sheely
ISBN 1 84310 717 1

Enabling Communication in Children with Autism
Carol Potter and Chris Whittaker
ISBN 1 85302 956 4

Asperger's Syndrome
A Guide for Parents and Professionals
Tony Attwood
ISBN 1 85302 577 1

Parenting a Child with Asperger Syndrome
200 Tips and Strategies
Brenda Boyd
ISBN 1 84310 137 8

Understanding Autism Spectrum Disorders
Frequently Asked Questions
Diane Yapko
ISBN 1 84310 756 2

Giggle Time – Establishing the Social Connection

A Program to Develop the Communication Skills of Children with Autism, Asperger Syndrome and PDD

Susan Aud Sonders

Jessica Kingsley Publishers
London and Philadelphia

Disclaimer
The author and publisher disclaim responsibility for any adverse effect resulting
directly or indirectly from the games described and illustrated herein,
or from the reader's misunderstanding of the text.

First published in the United Kingdom in 2003
by Jessica Kingsley Publishers
116 Pentonville Road
London N1 9JB, England
and
400 Market Street, Suite 400
Philadelphia, PA 19106, USA

www.jkp.com

Copyright © Susan Aud Sonders 2003
Illustrations copyright © Martin Sonders 2003
Second impression 2003
Reprinted twice in 2004

Library of Congress Cataloging in Publication Data
A CIP catalog record for this book is available from the Library of Congress

British Library Cataloguing in Publication Data
Sonders, Susan Aud, 1950-
    Giggle time : establishing the social connection / Susan Aud Sonders.
        p. cm.
    Includes bibliographical references and index.
    ISBN 1-84310-716-3 (pbk : alk paper)
    1. Autistic children--Education. 2. Language arts. 3. Interpersonal communication. 4. Autism in
children. I. Title.

LC4717.5 .S66 2002
371.94--dc21   2002028652

ISBN 1 84310 716 3

Printed and Bound in Great Britain by
Athenaeum Press, Gateshead, Tyne and Wear

Contents

To my mother, Sylvia, I've received through your eyes a picture
of all I can be. I've received through your love the courage to prevail.

To the hero of my heart, my husband Marty,
your love has cradled me, giving my spirit wings.

To all who despair,
May you find the gifts that are born there:
endurance, hope, patience, and faith.

Foreword

Susan Sonders' *Giggle Time – Establishing the Social Connection* presents practitioners with a method for employing play tutoring to scaffold communication skills in children with autism spectrum disorders. Play tutoring involves adults taking the initiative in structuring reciprocal playful interactions with children, that can be sustained, repeated, and varied over time. The ability to be an effective play tutor requires adults to be adept at structuring "play formats", successive rounds of repetitive turn-taking that clarify the "rules" of the game for both participants. Each of the games described in *Giggle Time* progresses through the verbatim repetition of a sequence of cues that become increasingly effective "triggers" of the contingent behaviors that maintain the play. As with all play tutoring, the adult bears the burden of adjusting the play's repetitive format based on the child's ongoing responses as the game unfolds. Ms Sonders' manual provides both specific instructions on how to structure each play activity, as well as rationales for decisions the play tutor must make when varying the turn-taking routine.

Giggle Time is both sophisticated in its application of play theory, and practical in its assumption that adults need guidance when improvising social play activities with children on the autism spectrum. In the section on the uses of rhyme to maintain participation, Ms Sonders illustrates how adults can capitalize on the rhythmic and rhymed structure of nursery rhymes to provide auditory cues that intensify and clarify the dramatic structure of the play. Using the Humpty Dumpty rhyme as an example she describes how the lines can be broken into shorter phrases and paired with actions to make the play more vivid and compelling for children. These suggestions are helpful because they provide detailed, practical information that supports adults attempts to perform social play with children who may have difficulty perceiving and conforming to the play format.

The guiding idea that runs through *Giggle Time* is that the ability to participate in mutually satisfying social play is a fundamental form of cultural literacy, which is foundational to all other communicative competencies. The book provides a blueprint for creating a curriculum that develops the crucial pragmatic communication skills of joint attention, reciprocity, and turn-taking that are the basis of pre-conversational speech. Ms Sonders rightly asserts that each giggle game is a highly enjoyable "mini conversation" that motivates children to remain in close proximity and maintain interaction. Susan Sonders' well organized and readable text is accompanied by photographs that clarify her directions for presenting and performing each game with children. Her approach to scaffolding pragmatic communication skills through contingency play is of great value to parents, teachers, and other professionals who work with young children on the autism spectrum.

Andrew Gunsberg,
Associate Professor of Early Childhood
Oakland University

Acknowledgments

With deepest gratitude, I thank the following.

My children, Jason and Lindsay Sutter, stepchildren, Jessica, Jennifer, and David Sonders, and godchild, Melanie Adie, for the many times I was unavailable as I typed in isolation. Thank you for the gift of time.

My sister, Marla Haller, and brothers, David and Ken Aud, mother-in-law, Esther and brothers-in-law, Nelson Sonders and Ron Haller, and sisters-in-law, MaryAnn and Jennie Aud, for their faith in me and for patiently forgiving my divided attention.

My beloved deceased father, Kenneth Aud, who encouraged me to enter the field of autism, and my deceased godfather, Carl Alfsen, who led me to believe I could reach any goal I set.

My friends and fellow professionals who encouraged me throughout this writing endeavor: Sue Kove, Jeanne Holmes, Sandee Hopcian, Marge Stoi, Lynn Baumann, Rose Anne Neppa, Denise Jackson, Connie Vallee, Jennifer Bartz, Sandy Biondo, Shirley Piatek, Gloria Conti, Tina Bommarito, Nancy Chrzanowski, AnMarie Filipeck, Linda Hodgon, Joyce Cheek, Dr Kathy Pistono, Dr Carol Swift, Marti Muss, Deanne Charron, Diana McCue, Marge Monarch, Nicole Mazzoline, Ray and Annette Azar, Karen Hicks, Angie Steiner, Melanie Shifflett, Maureen Gingrich and Dr Keyte.

The many wonderful families that I have worked with and whose children have been my inspiration.

Drs Stanley I. Greenspan, Andrew Gunsberg, James MacDonald, and Barry Prizant, whose thorough writings affirm to me the value of my work.

Is there ever any particular spot where one can put one's finger and say, it all began that day, at such a time and such a place, with such an incident.

Agatha Christie, *Each Day a New Beginning*

Introduction

The intervention that follows was created out of necessity. As I began to spend time with special needs children, I realized that I was a foreigner in uncharted land. I knew I had to toss away the familiar and sketch a new plan. With a heavy heart, I realized that I had no idea what that would be.

We all have had a moment when the answer we are seeking comes to us. It comes at just the right time in just the right way. It hits with a certainty that moves us forward with an air of confidence and the gift of knowing. That moment occurred when I heard a single idea: "The initial playground is small, six inches to one foot, and is between mother and child, long before the playground of toys."

I suddenly knew what was wrong. I had been introducing a playground of toys and activities to children who were not yet comfortable with the playground of people.

Walk with me through these pages and I will explain how I moved these children into the "initial playground" of people. As we played in this new playground, we developed "turn-taking" games. The playground of people soon impacted their social reciprocity, the development of significant pragmatic skills, and language acquisition. I named these sessions "Giggle Time" to remind myself of the primary goals: to engage children in turn-taking interactions that induced smiles, giggles, or belly laughs, to pin-point and shape emerging communication attempts and to show the child how wonderful it is to socially connect. (It is important to note that giggle time does not necessarily mean tickle time, since some children are highly sensitive to various intensities of touch. The play formats that develop in giggle time can end with any reinforcer that provides the goal of shared affect or the vital social connection.)

Each chapter is introduced with a "letter to Jacob." Even though the names in the letters and examples are fictitious, they exemplify the struggle that you and I have known as we have attempted time and time again to reach a particular child. For ease of reading, when children and adults are referred to in general, they are described as "he" or "she" rather than "he/she."

As these pages unfold, may you too find the right words at the right time. May they be words of encouragement to keep you going during times of frustration. May they provide clarity and spark as you journey with the children under your care and be of inspiration as you reach into the darkness and emerge as two, into the light.

> *I now intend to give the reader a short description of this country as far as I have travelled in it.*
>
> Jonathan Swift, *Gulliver's Travels*

1

Developing a Turn-Taking Sequence

CHAPTER OVERVIEW

This chapter will discuss the process of developing joint action routines between the child and adult. When the adult finds himself in a relationship with a child lacking the ability to attend in a reciprocal interaction, the child may also possess a core communication deficit in the area of joint attention. If the child lacks joint attention, he will not appear "social" despite the amount of language acquisition that has taken place. How does the adult develop the child's social connection from, what appears at first glance, nothing? We begin here.

Dear Jacob,

How do I reach you, sweet child? I have worked with you many times. Yet, I feel that we still have not met. I get a glimpse of you now and then but you continue to hide behind the many faces of autism.

Today I watched you momentarily before I approached. You were so pre-occupied with your own sounds and movements with your head down, running haphazardly, hand flapping, and screeching. It was unsettling. When I approached, you remained indifferent and quickly turned away. I called your name softly from behind, with no response. I stomped my feet, closely scrutinizing your every move and sound…no change. I felt invisible.

I called your name, stomped my feet and sang the first three words of your favorite rhyme, "Eensy Weensy Spider." Suddenly you stopped moving. A proud smile crossed my face. That was your first "turn." Now I could begin to shape your responses into meaningful social connections. A turn-taking sequence had begun. Over the next few months we will strive to socially connect in turn-taking sessions. It is there that we will meet and explore the world of laughter. The world of laughter is a different place. It's where we will let time pass slowly by and become lost in the sound of joy.

Love,

Miss Sue

Set your intentions high. Aim to be a saint and a miracle worker...
See the miracles around you and that will make it easier for greater
miracles to grow.

Deepak Chopra, *How to Know God*

WHAT IS A GIGGLE GAME?

KEY POINTS

Becoming the playground

A giggle time period consists of a ten-minute interaction between an adult and child.

A giggle game period consists of a ten-minute interval. During this time, the adult becomes the playground as he or she engages the child in roughhouse play routines. The primary goal of a giggle game is to build the social relationship between the child and the adult so that a rich, warm, natural environment is created where intentional communication can be shaped and joint attention can flourish.

While engaging, the adult and child build a sequence of communicative turns together. The adult looks for behaviors in the child that might be interpreted as communicative. He or she then shapes those behaviors by responding in an interesting way. Each response is called a "turn." Over the next few minutes, the adult continues to shape a series of movements, gestures, and vocalizations into communicative turns with the child. As this sequence develops, a beginning, middle, and end of the routine are formulated in the mind of the adult. Once formulated, it becomes a "giggle game" routine and is played repetitively until the ten-minute giggle time period ends.

Each giggle game has a beginning, middle and ending.

Giggle games are the basis of pre-conversational speech.

Giggle games are mini-conversations.

These turn-taking routines are the basis of pre-conversational speech. They are mini-conversations, with each partner taking a communicative turn and waiting for the turn of the other. Just as in a conversation, joint attention, staying in close proximity, enjoying each other's company and social reciprocity are involved.

LET'S IMAGINE

How to create a giggle game

EXAMPLE

The following giggle game is an example of how to capture the moment and create a spontaneous game out of the child's actions. It illustrates how a game consists of a series of turns, how the adult assigns meaning to the child's ordinary actions and how the game's beginning, middle and ending are formed. It illustrates how the turns are initially altered by the adult and child until a mutually agreed-upon sequence emerges.

PROBLEM

Marcus is very serious. Any attempt to formally engage him in a lap, floor, or sitting position results in resistance. He has a hyper responsive tactile system. He moves away when he thinks he's going to be touched. He is very active, having difficulty sitting for any length of time. He has very little staying power in a small play space and flees within seconds.

SOLUTION

Seize the moment and take advantage of an ordinary action that he exhibits. Construct a play space that temporarily expands and then closes up again, allowing him a feeling of safety and control as it expands and he flees. Give meaning to his moving/standing positions, forming them into turns. Use his movement *away* as one of his turns in the turn-taking sequence.

AHHHH

> The adult assigns meaning to the child's ordinary actions by making them turns in a giggle game.

Child: *Marcus has just turned to walk away from the adult once again. As he turns, his back is towards the adult. The adult begins to shape turning to walk away as a possible child's turn and the beginning of a giggle game.*

Adult: Ahhhhhh. *Begins softly and then becomes louder, with a building crescendo of sound.*

Use movement, such as the child walking away, as a turn in a giggle game.	**Child:** *Continuing to walk, is now three feet away. Walking away could be a possible child's turn and the middle of a giggle game.*
	Adult: *Grabs Marcus from behind and playfully pulls him down to the floor. This could be an adult's turn and possible ending if he demonstrates subtle pleasure or even passive acceptance.*
	Child: *Quiet, startled. No social smile. Gets back up and turns to walk away again. This action is the same turn that the adult gave meaning to before, and thus, the game repeats.*
The cessation of movement can also be a child's turn in a giggle game.	**Adult:** Ahhhhhh. *This is the same initial adult turn that worked favorably before.*
	Child: *Stops three feet away and waits. He is forming a new middle. He is beginning to anticipate the sequence of turns and demonstrate interest.*
	Adult: *Grabs Marcus and pulls him close for a tight bear hug. Adult is attempting to find a new ending. He did not like being pulled to the floor.*
The adult and child alter the game's beginning, middle and ending until a mutually agreed upon sequence develops.	**Child:** *Laughs. The new ending worked which is evident by the child's favorable response.*
	Adult: *Laughs and lets go of him.*
	Child: *Gets back up, begins to turn and walk away again. The beginning is consistently working and remains the same. Neither the adult nor the child has changed it.*

Adult: Ahhhhhh.

Child: *Stops, waits, turns head, looking over his shoulder and makes eye contact with adult. He has formed a new middle.*

Adult: *Grabs him and pulls him close for a tight bear hug. Same ending. Waiting for him to look over his shoulder before touching him makes this ending work, since he is hyper-sensitive to touch.*

Child: *Laughs.*

Adult: *Laughs and lets go of him.*

Sequence is repeated for ten minutes.

Ahhhhhhh

He's walking away from me again. Maybe this could be the **beginning** of a giggle game.

Ahhhhhhhhhh

What's that sound?

He stopped, waited, and then looked over his shoulder. Maybe this could be the **middle** of a giggle game.

He's laughing. This hug could be the **end** of a giggle game.

She caught me! Let's play again!

Since this child likes deep pressure, a tight bear hug is an effective reinforcer for this giggle game.

WHAT? WHEN? WHY?

Answers to common questions

Q. How do giggle games lay the foundation for conversational speech?

A. Until a child enjoys being near you, engages you in a back and forth manner and strains to keep you involved, the possibility of developing conversational speech is slim. Of course there are many variables that make up the development of conversational speech, but tools developed during giggle time are an integral piece of the foundation. Many of these tools come under the heading of "pragmatics" or pre-language skills. *Pragmatics* is the relationship between the speaker and listener. It is a system of social interaction that may or may not include speech. When speech is involved, it is the ability to use that language to communicate effectively. Staying in proximity of another, eye contact, joint attention, social smile, intentional gestures directed to another, movements, sounds, continuing an interaction, and taking turns communicating verbally and/or nonverbally are but a few. They lay the framework that conversational speech is built upon.

Q. Does that mean that, if my child develops giggle time routines, conversational speech will follow?

A. Not necessarily; however, the chances are far greater than if he never developed these skills. Through giggle time, whether or not "speech" develops, the child will become a communicator. He will no longer be lost in isolation but will seek out the company of others, happily engaging in social interaction.

Q. What about age-appropriate curriculum? Doesn't it look babyish to play infant games with pre-school children?

A. We must begin where the child is. It may appear babyish for a short time but the games will quickly evolve to a higher level as the child develops communicative skills.

Q. Why does a giggle game need a beginning, middle and an end?

A. It is imperative to the success of the game. With these three components in mind, a flow will develop in the routine; much like the flow between partners involved in conversational speech. With a particular beginning, middle and ending, it becomes a routine that can be played in the same way over a period of time. Without these components, the game continues endlessly and the child never experiences a sense of mastery since the climax or ending never takes place. Staying power would definitely be lost.

Q. Does this mean that the game never changes? It remains the same, one month, two months, and six months later?

A. No. Initially it is important for a sequence to emerge that doesn't change so that each partner knows and anticipates the other's turn. This produces a feeling of ease or "conversational flow." However, as the child's communicative skills develop, he may alter the giggle game by changing some of his turns. When this occurs, it is important to follow his lead, developing a variation of the game with the child. This is explained in greater detail in later chapters.

OBJECTIVES WORKSHEET

Build a number of giggle games

CHILD'S NAME_____

CURRENT LEVEL

The child is displaying difficulty building one or more play routines with an adult. The child leaves the area before one game is established and repeated. As the adult experiments with various turns, the child appears indifferent to the adult and the attempted interaction. It may be difficult to engage him and assign meaning to his sounds and movements because he appears passive or continually turns away, ready for flight. The child may have one game that he plays over and over but does not display interest in developing new ones.

Date initiated_____ Date mastered_____

1. Child will build a sequence of turns with an adult, forming one predictable giggle game with a beginning, middle and end.

Date initiated_____ Date mastered_____

2. Child will build three predictable giggle games with an adult, each with a beginning, middle and end.

Date initiated_____ Date mastered_____

3. Child will build five predictable giggle games with an adult, each with a beginning, middle and end.

What you and the child do is less important than finding something you can do in an enjoyable back and forth manner.

James MacDonald, *Becoming Partners with Children*

LOOKING FOR POSSIBLE TURNS

KEY POINTS

From nothing to something

> The adult assigns meanings to the child's behaviors by immediately playing an interesting turn.

> Accept the emergence of a communication goal as a turn.

> An adult's turn can be as simple as an exaggerated laugh, sudden movement, sound.

How does one begin with a child who appears to prefer isolation, screams when their personal space is invaded and has no apparent interest in developing a turn-taking sequence? The adult begins with one attempt after another until a sideways glance, a hesitation, a sound or a change in the child's expression is caught by the adult and reinforced as a turn.

At this point, the child is at a perlocutionary or pre-intentional communication level. The child is not yet aware that his behaviors can be interpreted as a form of communication. He does not anticipate social responses contingent upon his behavior, nor does he direct verbal or nonverbal signals to others. It is up to the adult to assign meaning to the child's potentially communicative behaviors, giving them intent. The adult gives them communicative intent by assigning meaning to random nonsymbolic behaviors. He can assign meaning by accepting the child's glance, hesitation, expression, smile or sound as a possible turn in a giggle game sequence. Through the adult's consistent responsiveness to a behavior, the child will learn that he can predictably affect another. He will be on his way to developing the ability to communicate.

LET'S IMAGINE

How to look for possible turns

EXAMPLE

The following giggle game is an example of an adult looking for possible turns on which to build a play routine.

PROBLEM

Spencer is enclosed in a playhouse, preferring to reside separately from classroom activities and people for long periods of time. Due to sensory defensiveness any attempt to socially engage him by removing him from the clubhouse is met with shrill screams. Attempting to join him in the clubhouse is met with further withdrawal to the sides of the house and a quick escape out of its door.

SOLUTION

Do not try to remove him from the playhouse or join him. Be unobtrusive around the perimeter of the playhouse and assign meaning to the child's incidental movements and expressions. Watch for the child's response. If it is favorable, keep it as a possible adult turn in the giggle game sequence.

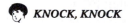

KNOCK, KNOCK

> *A startled expression can be a child's turn in a giggle game.*

Child: *Walking inside playhouse.*

Adult: *Kneels in front of door and knocks.*

Child: *Stops moving. Assign communicative meaning to the child's sudden lack of movement by making it his turn.*

Adult: *Slowly sings child's name.*

Child: *Glances toward door. Assign communicative meaning to child's eye gaze and make his glance his turn.*

Adult: *Throws the door open.*

Child: *Startled, alert, interested expression.*

Adult: *Lunges into playhouse with animated facial expression. This action assigns communicative meaning to the child's interested expression.*

Child: *Eye contact.*

Adult: *Tickles.*

Child: *Laughs.*

Knock Knock

Spencer ♫ ...

Spencer ♫ ...

Spencer ♫ ...

When an active child enters a closed area, take advantage of his inactivity and build a giggle game around it. Upon hearing his name, the child suddenly stops. The adult assigns meaning to the child's lack of movement by making his stillness a turn.

He glanced in my direction. I'll throw open the door.

The adult assigns meaning to the child's interested expression by quickly lunging into the playhouse.

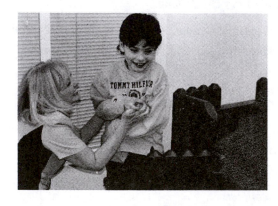

An element of surprise is often a successful ending for a giggle game.

WHAT? WHEN? WHY?

Answers to common questions

Q.   What if a tickle doesn't produce the desired effect?

A.   Try something else that the child might enjoy. A tossed scarf, a tackle to the ground, a spin, flip, noise blower, or a loud "Boo!" may prove to be effective. Remember that a child who is hypersensitive or defensive to touch, may prefer a heavy touch rather than a light touch. Look at the child's sensory issues.

Q.   How do you know which behavior should be assigned meaning? Which behavior do you choose?

A.   Choose one or more of the pragmatic pre-language skills that the child needs to acquire or demonstrate with higher frequency. Eye contact, gesture, movement, social smile, touch, proximity, or vocalizations are just a few.

Q.   What if the child's turn is only a quick sideways glance, a hesitation or a startled response?

A.   You must begin where the child is. Be patient and accept emerging pragmatic skills as a possible turn right now by assigning meaning to it.

Q.   How do you get the child to do a pragmatic skill or an emergence of a skill on his turn? He is ignoring me.

A.   The child is purposefully trying to ignore you. Dr Stanley Greenspan states that ignoring "is a form of interaction, for it is an acknowledgment of your presence. Given this acknowledgment, you have a chance to build a longer, more positive, interaction." Imitate him, and when the opportunity presents itself "be playfully obtrusive." Dr Greenspan states that you can "playfully insert yourself in a way that makes it harder for him to ignore you." Gradually work your way into his attention. Get a step ahead and arrange a collision. Attempt various obtrusions. Ignoring is a "purposeful response" and is the beginning of an interaction (Greenspan 1998).

OBJECTIVES WORKSHEET

Demonstrate ability to take one of several possible turns

CHILD'S NAME_____

CURRENT LEVEL

This child is at a pre-intentional communication level. The majority of his sounds, babbles, and movements are not purposeful or directed to someone. They are random. An example of a random movement might be a sudden fling of an arm that might be shaped into a child's turn. Building a turn-taking sequence upon this child's sounds is difficult since he may have only one or two in his repertoire. Eye contact is fleeting and evidence of a social smile may require a great amount of diligence on the part of the adult. The child may be extremely passive or demonstrate agitation and distress when his personal space is intruded upon.

Date initiated_____ Date mastered_____

1. Child will take a turn during a giggle time routine with an adult by indicating one or more of the following: smile, touch, eye contact, or gesture. (Adult looks for these behaviors to shape into a meaningful turn in the game.)

Date initiated_____ Date mastered_____

2. Child will take a turn during a giggle time routine with an adult by making any movement. (Adult assigns communicative intent to any movement, shaping it into a meaningful turn in the game.)

Date initiated_____ Date mastered_____

3. Child will take a turn during a giggle time routine with an adult by making a sound, babble, word approximation or vocalization. (Adult assigns meaning to any sound by making it a meaningful turn in the game.)

Participation in simple contingency play formats with an adult cultivates an appetite for playful interactions in children whose previous modes of interaction were either hostile or avoiding.

Andrew Gunsberg, *Childhood Education*

BUILDING A SEQUENCE OF TURNS

KEY POINTS

Keeping it predictable

The adult's turn must be the same length as the child's turn. If too many turns are taken or the adult's are longer, the child's interest will be lost.

In a "giggle game," each player's behavior becomes contingent upon the behavior of the other. If the adult's behavior is interesting, it triggers an emerging communicative behavior in the child. The observant adult quickly catches this behavior and accepts it as the child's turn. The way he accepts it is by playing another interesting turn. This, in turn, triggers another turn from the child. Now, four turns have taken place and a ten-minute routine is well on its way to being established.

A giggle game is a predictable series of turns.

A giggle game is not just a series of turns. It is a *predictable* series of turns between adult and child. Remember the goal of a "giggle time" session; to develop a play routine between adult and child that is repetitively played for ten minutes. In order to do this, the turns must be predictable. They become predictable when the adult repeats his turns exactly the same way each time. He must think back to his previous turns and the specific actions that triggered the child's responses.

The child will begin to anticipate the adult's turn if the sequence is played exactly the same way each time.

Those turns may have included animated facial expression, voice volume, inflection, exaggerated body movement, sounds or words. Repeating turns in the same way each time causes the child to anticipate and predict what the next turn will be. Only through exact repetition of the sequence will the child discover the rules of the game. "When I do this_____, she always does that_____." Dr Andrew Gunsberg states that ease or "conversational flow" can only be accomplished through "verbatim repetition" (Gunsberg 1989).

LET'S IMAGINE

A series of turns played exactly the same way

EXAMPLE

The following giggle game is an example of an adult creating a series of turns with a child. Remember that the play routine must be repeated over and over again in exactly the same way once it is built. Thus, it is imperative that the number of turns in a routine be limited so that each turn can be easily remembered.

PROBLEM

Kenny is very passive. He is often found on the floor gazing intently at various angles and patterns. He appears to enjoy the sensation of pressure and position of body in space that lying on the floor provides. He is nonverbal and rarely vocalizes sounds. Eye contact is fleeting.

SOLUTION

Imitate the child's body posture, lay down very closely to narrow the play space between you. Move quietly and gently. Use very little language. Incorporate a soft touch, soothing voice, an object prop, and an element of surprise into the routine. Watch closely for any subtle movements or sounds that may be interpreted as a series of turns for the child. Since he has a need for visual stimulation, change the visual field by covering and uncovering his head with a blanket. The blanket will also provide enclosure, a close feeling providing security.

NIGHT-NIGHT

Eye contact, movement, babbling sounds and laughter can be an adult's turn in the turn-taking sequence.	**Child:** *Lying on floor, eye contact. Eye contact can be a turn.* **Adult:** *Lies next to child on floor, strokes child's head and loosely covers child's head with blanket.* "Night, night." **Child:** *Moves under blanket. Movement can be a turn.*

Eye contact, movement, babbling sounds and laughter can be a child's turn in the turn-taking sequence.

Adult: *Partially closes eyes, snores with exaggeration, twice. Second snore is very slow.*

Child: *Babbling sound. Soft babble can be a turn.*

Adult: Good morning! *Adult suddenly pulls blanket off child.*

Child: *Laughs.*

Night-night

As the adult builds a sequence of predictable turns with this child, she imitates his body posture and keeps the play space between them very small. She watches for subtle movements, eye contact, or sounds that she can interpret as turns.

WHAT? WHEN? WHY?

Answers to common questions

Q. I feel so confused and lost at the beginning as I attempt to develop a turn-taking routine with a child. Is this normal?

A. Yes! I feel it every time I am engaged in the development of a new routine. Try not to panic. It is just like a conversation with a friend. Neither of you know where the conversation is going but when you are finished, the outcome is what the two of you have created together. I'm sure the child is confused at the beginning as well. That is why exact repetition is so important. Through repetition, each person anticipates the other's turn and confusion turns into clarity.

Q. How will I know if the child liked my turn? He shows so little expression.

A. This is very common. Many times the child's expression doesn't change until the sequence is repetitively played and suddenly you are amazed at how much he loves the game! It is easier to note if the child does not like your turn. Watch for a turn of the body away from you, aversion of eye gaze and, more obvious, screaming or walking away.

Q. What is an indication of interest so that I know if I should keep a particular turn?

A. A second of eye gaze, remaining in proximity, emergence of a smile, a sideways glance, alertness to your presence, a quick turn of the head in your direction, and becoming momentarily still are all indications of interest.

Q. How many turns should be in a turn-taking routine?

A. As little as two or as many as you both create. Remember, the adult's turns must be repeated *exactly* each time the sequence is played. Its success will depend on your memory!

Q. When should my turns be repeated exactly?

A. Your turns must be repeated *exactly* once you have finished making up the game with the child. Before that period, your turns should be continually altered depending on the response of the child. The child's interest is continually assessed the first time your turns are played. If interest is displayed, that turn is kept. If attention decreases, that turn is altered and then tried again. Once the routine is set and it is mutually acceptable to both you and the child, your turns are repeated exactly so that the child has an opportunity to display a growing sense of expectancy. Verbatim repetition enables him to predict your turn, which is crucial for the development of conversational flow.

Q. Why do I have to formulate my turns quickly? It's hard to do when a giggle game is being created.

A. If the pace isn't fast, the child will lose interest and walk away. Quickly formulate and alter your turns. When you feel the need to alter a turn, don't spend a lot of time thinking about it. Just do what you just did, but *a little* different.

Q. How will I know if the turn-taking sequence is a success?

A. You will know with every cell of your being. The child will momentarily gaze deep into your eyes and you will experience him in a way you have never before. There will be a sense of intimacy between you. The routine will flow freely and all other thoughts in your head will disappear. You will connect, heart to heart, and you will radiate with gratitude born of this connection.

OBJECTIVES WORKSHEET

Demonstrate interest in a sequence of turns

CHILD'S NAME _____

CURRENT LEVEL

This child may appear uninterested in building a series of interactive turns with the adult. He may even leave the area, wishing to be free to pursue his own interests. Eye contact may be minimal and fleeting as the adult attempts to build a play routine with the child. A slight movement of the eye in the adult's direction may be a starting-point for one turn. The adult must closely scrutinize the child for any change in body posture, immediately react to it, and assign communicative meaning. The adult must listen intently for even the softest sound, quickly making it one of the child's turns.

Date initiated_____ Date mastered_____

1. Given the building of a giggle time routine, the child will demonstrate interest in the adult's turns through slight body movements and/or facial awareness.

Date initiated_____ Date mastered_____

2. Given the building of a giggle time routine, the child will demonstrate interest in the adult's turns by remaining in close proximity to the adult.

The solution is never at the level of the problem – the solution is always love, which is beyond problems.

Deepak Chopra, *The Path to Love*

ALTERING YOUR TURN

KEY POINTS

I'm trying but he's not responding

> You are both the teacher and the student as you develop a sequence.

> The giggle time routine must be mutually satisfying.

> Watch the child's eyes, mouth and body posture closely to see if your turn was effective.

> If the child is not interested, your turn is not working.

> Drop what is not working; keep what is.

Perhaps you entered the turn taking with a preconceived notion of what your turn might be. It is imperative to remember that you are building a social routine together. As it is built together, a routine will emerge that is specific to the two personalities involved. You must be flexible and willing to alter your preconceived turns. One way to alter your turn is to pretend that 12 variations of your turn are possible. Variations might include the addition of a prop, sudden movement, and element of surprise, exaggerated sound or inflection. Or, you might try pulling the child's feet rather than wiggling them. Play each variation until you get a flicker of interest from the child, keeping that turn and working on your next turn. If interest is received, place that turn into the developing routine sequence. Each time you are met with lack of interest, slightly alter that turn.

After some turns have been kept and some discarded, the sequence will be set. Then the sequence is repetitively played for ten minutes. The repetition will turn the child's flicker of interest into a flame.

LET'S IMAGINE
_____

Altering your turn

EXAMPLE

The following example demonstrates how the adult must continually alter his turn in order to build a successful game with the child. When a child does not show even a subtle sign of interest, the adult must alter his turn *slightly* and then observe the child closely to see if that turn had a favorable impact. If the child did not react favorably, the adult must try again and again. There will be giggle time periods that feel like it's nothing more than one altered turn after another. That's OK. Be persistent and playful and keep trying. Watch the child closely for cues during the other parts of the day. Think of the sensory and motor sensations that the child does like and try introducing them into a game.

PROBLEM

Conrad displays very little eye contact, low muscle tone, and his facial expression rarely expresses pleasure. With low tone and lacking body orientation in space, he often lies on the floor or is found at the perimeter of the room, hugging the wall. He enjoys joint compression. Appearing to be hyposensitive, he has an under-responsiveness to touch. He is currently nonverbal, with no vocalizations. His staying power is one to two minutes in an interaction. He appears aloof and uneasy, often moving quickly away from any attempted interaction.

SOLUTION

Keep the play small, between six and twelve inches, to encourage eye contact. Stand and bend over him so that your heads are close together. Make a game out of the body position he is in; laying on the floor. Incorporate jerky movement to provide heavy input into the joints. In case he is gravitational insecure, remain on the floor to provide a sense of position in space for security. Keep the giggle game sequence short. Watch for very subtle cues of a slight turn of the head, fleeting eye contact, and remaining in proximity as indications of interest. Keep language at a minimum, using only key words.

 *READY…SET…GO!*

> Child: *Laying on floor, on back, no eye contact.*
>
> Adult: *Stands over child. Takes his feet in hands.*

> The adult altered one of her turns three times while building this giggle game with the child.

Child: *No eye contact, no movement. No response to adult's turn.*

Adult: *Alters this turn by jiggling child's feet, three seconds.*

Child: *No response.* [*Alter next turn.*]

Adult: *Suddenly jerks child by feet and pulls him three to four inches.*

Child: *No response.* [*Alter next turn.*]

Adult: *Suddenly jerks child by feet, pulling him three to four inches, this time adding word to accompany movement:* Ready?

Child: *One second of eye contact. This can become his turn. Keep previous adult turn that triggered this response and begin formulating the next adult turn.*

Adult: *Continues to hold on to feet and pull him in a zigzag pattern across the floor.* S...e...t, *said slowly.*

Child: *Eye contact. This can be his turn. Keep previous adult turn that triggered this response and begin formulating the next adult turn.*

Adult: Go!, *said loudly. Adult holds feet and pulls child quickly in a straight line.*

Child: *Eye contact, smiles.*

What is the routine that developed after the child displayed disinterest and the adult altered her turns? Let's review.

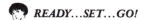 *READY...SET...GO!*

Child: *Lying on floor, on back.*

Adult: *Suddenly jerks child by feet and pulls him three to four inches.* Ready?

Child: *Eye contact.*

Adult: *Continues to hold feet and pulls child in a zigzag pattern across the floor, speaking slowly.* S...e...t.

Child: *Eye contact.*

Adult: GO! *This is said loudly while holding on to the child's feet and pulling him quickly in a straight line.*

Child: *Eye contact, smiles.*

The altered sequence is repeated for ten minutes.

Ready...Set...Go!

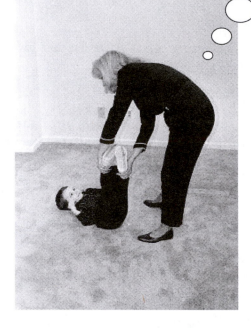

He didn't respond with interest to the jiggling or sudden jerking of his feet. I'll try pulling him by his feet a few inches.

Keep altering the adult's turn until interest is noted by the child's response.

WHAT? WHEN? WHY?

Answers to common questions

Q. Why did you attempt to create a routine while the child was lying on the floor, on his back?

A. You must make a game out of what the child is doing. This position also encourages eye contact as the adult stands and bends over the child. This position also decreases the play space, increasing the chances of a successful interaction.

Q. How do you "slightly" alter your turn?

A. Don't throw away the entire turn and start fresh. Just change it slightly. If a scarf is used as a prop and you're not receiving interest, don't put away the scarf. Try a variety of things with it. Throw it in the air, place it on the child's head, place it on your head and blow it off, hide it under his shirt. If you have the child's feet and you are not receiving interest, jiggle them, pull them, clap them together, hide behind them, or lift them up. If the child is in a box or fort, lean over it, knock on it, throw a sheet over it, push your hands quickly through the window, crawl around it quietly or jump up on a new side. In other words, do not "throw out" the turn, but alter as needed.

Q. What else can I do to alter my turn?

A. Increase your affect. Increase your enthusiasm, your playfulness, and your energy. Slow down, then increase, your movement. Soften your voice, and then make it louder. Exaggerate your facial expressions.

OBJECTIVES WORKSHEET

Remain engaged as turns are altered

CHILD'S NAME_____

CURRENT LEVEL

This child now enjoys, or at least tolerates, the initial few turns of a developing routine. However, any attempt to alter or lengthen the routine is met with difficulty. His staying power is still very weak. Any lull in the joint action routine is perceived as "the end" and he attempts to leave quickly. The pace of the developing routine must be fast so that his opportunity to leave is minimized. The adult must quickly alter and evaluate, with speed, further turns that may be of possible interest to this child.

Date initiated_____ Date mastered_____

1. Given a giggle game that is being built and altered, the child will communicate lack of interest in the adult's turns by a slight change in body posture, proximity, and/or head movement.

Date initiated_____ Date mastered_____

2. Given a giggle game that is being built and altered, the child will demonstrate satisfaction with the emerging routine through increased eye contact, social smile, and/or body movement.

Date initiated_____ Date mastered_____

3. Child will remain in proximity of adult for ten minutes while altering and developing a giggle game routine with adult.

When you feel a new impulse, an uplifting thought, an insight that you have never acted upon before, embrace the unknown. Cherish it as tenderly as a newborn baby... God lives in the unknown.

Deepak Chopra, *How to Know God*

THREE COMPONENTS OF SUCCESSFUL TURN-TAKING

KEY POINTS

After a few turns, I lose him

> Conversational flow develops when a predictable sequence, cue, and reinforcing turn are established.

> The "cue" is an exaggerated turn and is totally different from the other adult turns.

> The "cue" is played the same way and at the same time with each repetition.

> The reinforcing turn is at the end and is the last adult turn in a giggle game sequence.

Developing a successful sequence of turns not only involves a *predictable sequence*, but the development of a *cue* and a *reinforcing turn* as well. These three components play an essential role in shaping a "giggle time" routine. As turns are developed, the adult decides which turn will be cued and then experiments with the make-up of the reinforcing turn.

What is a cue? As a routine sequence draws to a close, the adult cues the child. The "cue" is the adult turn that is noticeably different from his other turns. It is exaggerated – louder, quieter, slower, or faster than any other adult turn in the sequence. With the inclusion of a cued turn, the sequence of the routine becomes clear and predictable to the child. Since it is predictable, it builds anticipation. It is always the second-to-last adult turn of the sequence. The cue tells the child that the end of the turn-taking sequence is drawing near and that what follows is the last, or "fun," turn that the child has been waiting for.

The "fun" turn is the reinforcing turn, the last turn that the adult plays in the sequence. It is the turn that makes the child love the routine and prompts his desire to play repetitively. It is the turn that the child has learned to expect, the reason he remains engaged and in proximity.

How do you know which turn will be the strongest reinforcer for the child? "Giggle time" does not necessarily mean "tickle time." If the child is not hypersensitive to touch and enjoys being tickled, then tickling may be the appropriate reinforcing turn for that child. When seeking an ending to a game, however, it is important to find a reinforcing turn that results in *shared affect*. As the adult formulates his turns, it is important for him to observe the child's reactions and watch for the stimulus that produces the most interest and positive affect from the child. This turn, the reinforcing turn, is then noted and becomes the ending of the routine.

A turn-taking sequence develops without a predetermined path. As such, the initial phase of building a sequence may be unsettling to the adult, since he is not in total control. Consider this analogy. Imagine walking up a mountain with the child. As the climb begins, it seems like the perfect way to spend time together. The initial steps are nice but you might feel unsettled, not quite sure of the path you're on. Initially there are small obstacles in the way and there may be some retracing of your path. This unsettled feeling is what the beginning of a turn-taking sequence is like as turns are tried and altered. As you proceed up the mountain and get closer to the top, you begin to anticipate what will be found. The air begins to electrify and excitement builds. This is what the "cue" feels like. Finally, the top is reached, and it is as beautiful as anticipated. This is the "reinforcer," and comes at the end of the journey. It becomes evident that the climb was worth every step. You wouldn't mind starting back at the foot of the mountain and proceeding upward, just to get to this spot again. It is also why the child continually repeats a giggle game sequence with you. He will want to get to the reinforcing turn again; to the top again, with you.

The "cued" turn tells the child that the end of the routine is coming.

The "reinforcing" turn is the turn that the child waits for throughout the sequence since it is fun.

LET'S IMAGINE

Three components of successful turn-taking

EXAMPLE

The following example demonstrates how crucial it is to incorporate the cue, reinforcing turn and predictable sequence into each giggle game. The first example, Rolling Chair, is comprised of the three components. The second example is deliberately missing one or more of these components so that you can see how its absence impacts the game.

PROBLEM

Jason is often seen twirling in circles, craving vestibular input. He also climbs under mats, buries himself in the pool of balls and squeezes between every object and the wall, causing quite a path of disarray. He lacks staying power, quickly moving away from adults. There is a lack of eye contact and babbling is heard intermittently.

SOLUTION

Incorporate intense movement into his giggle games. Experiment with a reinforcing turn that delivers heavy input into the joints and muscles. Place him on a piece of equipment that provides vestibular movement and build the game around it to aid his staying power. Also, keep the play space small for a portion of the game.

ROLLING CHAIR

> Every giggle game should have a predictable sequence, a cue and a reinforcing turn.

Child: *Establishes proximity to a rolling chair.*

Adult: *Places child in rolling chair, bends forward face to face, developing a play space of six to twelve inches.*

Child: *Child remains but no eye contact.*

Adult: Round and round and round we go, where we stop... *Quickly spins child clockwise in chair one time (predictable sequence).*

Child: *Smiles.*

> Pairing the slow pace of the chair's circular movement with the adult's slow utterances enhances the cue.

Adult: N...o...b...o...d...y k...n...o...w...s (*cue*). *Phrase is stated slowly, with heavy inflection while chair is also moved slowly.*

The reinforcer of wrestling the child out of the chair meets this child's sensory needs.	Child: *Babbling sound.* Adult: *Wrestles child out of chair with a bear hug* (*reinforcer*). Child: *Laughs.*

Sequence is repeated for ten minutes, alternating clockwise and counter-clockwise spinning direction in the rolling chair.

Rolling Chair

Round and round and round we go. Where we stop...

Predictable sequence

N...o...b...o...d...y   k...n...o...w...s

Cue

Reinforcer – the impact of wrestling the child from the chair to the floor provides sudden movement and input into the joints, alerting the vestibular and proprioceptive systems.

LET'S IMAGINE

What's missing? – Predictable sequence? Cue? Reinforcer?

EXAMPLE

The following example demonstrates a procedure for developing a giggle game.

PROBLEM

In any giggle game, a predictable sequence, cue and reinforcer are not added immediately. They evolve slowly as the game emerges. The adult must stay attuned to what component is still missing and needs to be inserted into the routine so that it is successful.

SOLUTION

As the following example is read, determine which components of a successful turn-taking routine are missing and still need to be inserted. Is it the cue, a predictable sequence or reinforcing turn?

 ROWBOAT

Child: *Sitting in rowboat.*

Adult: *Bends over opposite end of rowboat, rocks the boat and sings entire "Row Boat" song.*

Child: *Remains in boat, no eye contact, lack of social smile. When song has ended, sits for a few seconds and then climbs out of boat.*

What's wrong? A balanced sequence of turn taking is not evident. The adult's turn was too long. The child's turns were unclear.

> The adult takes a turn that is longer than the child's and loses his staying power.

Solution? Break down the adult's turns into smaller units and add some turns for the child.

Child: *Sitting in rowboat.*

Adult: *Bends over opposite end of row boat, rocks the boat and sings the first five words of "Row Boat" song instead song in entirety.*

Child: *Remains in boat, no eye contact, no apparent interest.*

Each time the ending word of a phrase is sung, the adult momentarily suspends the child up high in the rowboat. This provides the child with an opportunity to take a turn

Adult: *Sings first five words again as he rocks the boat but as the last word "boat" is sung, the adult pushes down on his end of the boat, suspending the child, up high, in his seat.*

Child: *Sideways glance, interest.*

Adult: *Begins rocking boat again and singing the rest of the phrase.* Gently down the stream. *When the last word, "stream," is sung, the adult pushes down on his end of the boat again. Once again the child is suspended.*

Child: *Eye contact.*

The sudden movement of the game prop is implemented at the same point in the giggle game each time it is played, which helps provide a predictable sequence.

Adult: Merrily, merrily, merrily, merrily. *Continues to rock the boat, suspending child on last word.*

Child: *Eye contact.*

Adult: Life is but a dream. *Continues rocking the boat, suspending child once again on last word (predictable sequence).*

Child: *Eye contact.*

What's wrong? The cue is missing. Even though clear adult and child turns and a predictable sequence are building, there is not an adult turn that signals to the child that the ending of the routine is near.

Solution? Make one adult turn exaggerated and different from the others.

The building of a predictable sequence, cue and reinforcing turn do not develop right away. It may take six or seven minutes of altered turns for an effective giggle game to emerge.

Adult: *Keep child suspended in air. Slowly sing.* Mer…ri…ly, mer…ri…ly, mer…ri…ly, mer…ri…ly. *Accent each syllable with a jerk of the boat (cue).*

Child: *Startled, interest, sustained eye contact.*

What's wrong? The reinforcing turn that the adult plays is missing.

Solution? Add an ending turn of what the child loves. Think about his sensory needs and what he often seeks out.

Adult: Life is but a dream! *Adult quickly sings, lunges in and tickles.*

Child: *Uneasy, shifted body away.*

Adult: (*Alter*) Life is but a dream! *Adult quickly sings, throws a sheet over the rowboat, enfolding the child. Firmly tosses child back and forth in the sheet as "dream" is sung (reinforcer).*

Child: *Laughs.*

Sequence is repeated for ten minutes.

WHAT? WHEN? WHY?

Answers to common questions

Q. What are some examples of cueing the play?

A. Whisper softly, talk louder, crouch low, jump up high, tip-toe softly, stomp heavily, run toward the child, march, clap, jingle a bell, pound something slowly or fast, throw something in the air, throw your head back and laugh loudly, sneeze with exaggeration, make a long "Ahh" sound, slow down or speed up a phrase of a rhyme. Whatever makes that turn *noticeably different* from your other turns.

Q. What else should I remember when I cue the routine?

A. Each time the giggle game sequence is played, the cue must be played in exactly the same way. Body posture, gestures, exaggerated expression and the tone of voice must be identical in every repetition.

Q. What is the main turn that keeps the child engaged in the interaction?

A. The reinforcer. The child goes along with the giggle game because they know that it is a build-up to the main attraction: the adult's last turn.

Q. Isn't each adult turn a reinforcing turn?

A. Yes, each time you respond to an emerging skill with an interesting turn you are reinforcing the previous behavior. However, the ending reinforcing turn is not just what interests the child. It is what the child *loves*.

Q. How long does it take to develop a turn-taking routine with a child and determine the sequence of turns, the cue and the ending reinforcer?

A. It may take six or seven minutes but it will feel much longer. Initially you will struggle to reach a *mutually satisfying* sequence of turns. Then you must figure out which turn to cue and experiment with an ending reinforcing turn.

Q. What are some examples of a reinforcing turn at the end of a sequence?

A. It can be physical: tickles, toss, tackle, spin or twirl. It can be verbal: a favorite phrase of a book, a letter or number.

Q. What about a child who has a hypersensitive tactile system?

A. He may allow firm rather than light touch. A firm tackle to the ground, hand squeeze or even a body wrap in a blanket may be acceptable. A deep touch, like a bear hug, could be worked into the routine. Widening the play space between the child and adult throughout the turn taking may be necessary for a while. As social routines develop and comfort levels increase, tactile defensiveness will decrease. Incorporating vestibular movement into the routine may help repair the tactile system. This is discussed in detail in Chapter 2.

Q. What else should I remember when I develop a reinforcing turn?

A. The reinforcing turn has an element of surprise. Since the cue has led to a build-up of excitement and exaggeration, the reinforcer can be startling and surprising.

Q. Do I have to accept a child's negative behavior as a turn?

A. No, ignore what you don't want the child to repeat. This is one reason why you must watch the child very closely and react very quickly with your turn. If you see the emergence of a pragmatic skill, you must react quickly with your turn before the child attaches to it another behavior which could be inappropriate. If you are not fast enough, you may reinforce that chain of behaviors and the child will repeat this chain to get the desired response from you. Also, if you played an interesting turn immediately after an undesirable behavior, the likelihood of his repeating it is high since it was reinforced. He will repeat it again to get the same response from you. Do not fertilize the weeds, only the flowers. However, the flowers may be hard to see. They may be tiny and without color. If a glance, turn of the head, eye gaze, babble, or slight movement appears as though it could be a flower, accept it, nurture it and reinforce it with your turn. It may surprise you and bloom.

Q. How will I remember the sequence of turns, the cue and the reinforcing turn tomorrow, next week or next month?

A. Immediately after the giggle time session, write out the child's turns and the adult's turns. Note the cue, reinforcing turn and title as well. The title will enable the child to receptively identify the routine and is one way he can initiate it if he has some expressive language. Note the Giggle Game worksheet provided for this purpose can be found at the back of the book in the Appendix.

OBJECTIVES WORKSHEET

Remain engaged when three components of successful turn-taking are in place

CHILD'S NAME _____

CURRENT LEVEL

This child's interest in playing joint action routines with an adult is new and in the emerging stage. His staying power is still weak. He has a few giggle games that he enjoys playing with staff, but the duration of each is not very long. He does not yet remain engaged for ten minutes. He needs repetitive exposure to a few completed giggle games so that he will begin to anticipate forthcoming turns. This will heighten his interest in remaining engaged with an adult for an extended period of time.

Date initiated_____ Date mastered_____

1. Given a giggle time routine with a predictable sequence, cue and reinforcing turn, the child will repetitively play the routine with an adult for ten minutes.

Date initiated_____ Date mastered_____

2. Given a giggle time routine with a predictable sequence, cue and reinforcing turn, the child will demonstrate anticipation of the adult's turns through heightened affect, vocalization, and/or sustained eye contact.

2

Developing Staying Power

CHAPTER OVERVIEW

Children who "have limited social 'staying power' reduce their opportunities to communicate and build relationships" (Young 1988). In giggle time, staying power is crucial and demonstrates itself in the child's ability to remain in close proximity of an adult for ten minutes while a game is being developed and repetitively played. If the child is not able to remain engaged for at least ten minutes, the chances of developing social reciprocity and communicative behaviors are slim. This chapter will discuss crucial tools which will aid the adult in keeping the child within close range for a specified amount of time.

Dear Jacob,

The gains that brought tears to my eyes yesterday are a distant memory today as I watch you slip from me once again. It is so hard to have faith in the unseen, working toward goals that appear elusive. They seem to be within reach one day and lost from my grasp the next.

I can't seem to keep you with me. You are turning away, walking away, and running away. Today you were not interested in the giggle time routine that we developed yesterday. You wanted to move quickly through the room, tapping, climbing and galloping. As I moved with you, I wasn't sure that you knew I was there. Suddenly I noted a sideward glance and caught the emergence of a smile. It was just what I needed to pull me back toward focused determination.

You will learn to stay engaged with me. I will continually watch for signs of interest and alter my actions to keep your interest kindled.

We will continue to strive to meet your goals. However, I am finding that it is in the journey that real learning takes place.

Love,

Miss Sue

Like an old gold-panning prospector, you must resign yourself to digging up a lot of sand from which you will later patiently wash out minute particles of gold ore.

Dorothy Bryant, *Each Day a New Beginning*

FOLLOWING THE CHILD'S LEAD

KEY POINTS

Lose him? Follow him!

> *Staying power is the ability to remain with an adult in a reciprocal interaction for ten minutes.*

> *The adult must watch, interpret and respond to the child's sounds and movements.*

> *Follow the child's lead and he will guide you. The child must develop 50 percent of the game.*

> *Following the lead of the child involves choosing a sound or movement and turning it into the beginning of a silly game that two can play.*

Giggle time is a child-oriented approach that involves "following the lead" of the child for a minimum of ten minutes. Many language intervention approaches caution against adult-directed interactions and emphasize child-oriented approaches. Fey (1986) described three steps in a child-oriented approach designed to follow the child's lead:

> …wait for the child to initiate some behavior; interpret that behavior as communicative and meaningful, and respond to that behavior in a manner that will facilitate further communicative interaction and language learning.

These three steps are incorporated into each giggle session. When engaged in the process of developing a turn taking, autistic children often initiate behaviors that are pre-intentional or without communicative intent. Picking up or standing near an object, fleeting eye gaze toward a person or object, a sound, reach, or slight turn of the head are a few examples of behaviors that may be interpreted. It is up to the adult to give meaning to pre-intentional behaviors by quickly responding with a turn that is interesting to the child. The child then understands that his behaviors impact

A child with little staying power will move throughout the room while one attempts to engage him. Follow him!

Following a lead gives the adult an opportunity to develop their creativity as new turns are manufactured and attempted.

Following the child's lead means watching the child's body language for evidence of disinterest and then not repeating the turn that caused it.

the world around him and the process of becoming a communicator begins.

However, following the lead of the child is difficult. As educators and parents, we are continually presented with models of how to engage children with a variety of directed play ideas and language patterns. We have past experience with this type of interaction and feel comfortable with it. Following the lead of a child for ten minutes feels very different. The adult must give up control. He must be free to experience what the child can bring to the interaction. Close monitoring of the child's faint and loud sounds as well as his subtle and gross movements will show the adult what the child can do. Following the lead of the child involves choosing one of these sounds or movements and attempting to turn it into the beginning of a silly game that two can play. It involves following the child's lead again if the silly game fails to develop. It involves choosing yet another sound or movement and attempting to assign meaning to it by responding with another interesting turn. Following a lead may even involve a great deal of movement throughout the room, especially if the child abruptly stands and runs away! When this happens, it is imperative for the adult to quickly follow the child to his next destination or activity.

Actively following the child's lead around the room can be mentally and physically exhausting. It can last the entire ten minutes and can even continue to be the make-up of giggle time over the next few months. However, the child's staying power will eventually change and may be so slow in coming that you may not be conscious of it improving. However, one day you will suddenly realize that following the child's movement throughout the room or from object to object is not occurring as often during a session. You will suddenly find that he is beginning to enjoy you, as evidenced by an increase in sustained eye contact, proximity and social smile.

LET'S IMAGINE

How to follow the child's lead while developing a giggle game

EXAMPLE

The following is an example of how to develop a giggle game by following the lead of a child. Paying close attention to both his subtle and overt body language follows the child's lead. Every movement and expression, no matter how slight, will give the adult information as to whether to proceed or stop. If the child displays any agitation or movement away, the adult must stop. He then watches the child closely and tries other interactive turns.

PROBLEM

Tommy prefers to be alone seeking out visual sensations. He is often found turning objects around in his hands or posturing his body so that he can look at things from unusual angles. He is most often found wandering the room. His staying power is 10 to 20 seconds when approached by an adult for interaction.

SOLUTION

Follow his lead by trying to make a giggle game out of an object he is manipulating. Try a variety of silly actions with the object on your turn. Try placing the object at varying angles providing visual input. Toss it in the air. Hide it in his sock. Bounce it off your head. Pair these quick movements with an exaggerated sound for interest. Remember that his turns may simply be remaining in proximity or slight eye gaze at this point. Let him take the lead by displaying interest or disinterest in your turn. Follow this lead by keeping or changing your turn. Monitor him closely, adjust accordingly and keep the play space very small (12 inches). Follow his movement around the room as needed.

 FOLLOWING THE LEAD TURNS INTO CHOO-CHOO TRAIN

> The adult follows the child's lead by making a giggle game out of the object he is manipulating.

> When the child turns his body away, the adult alters her turn.

Child: *Lying on back on floor holding puzzle piece.*

Adult: *Places feet on either side of child's body, bends over child and taps puzzle piece three times.* One, two, three!

Child: *Turns body away, on side. Holds puzzle piece.*

Adult: *Picks up puzzle piece and hides it loosely under child's shirt.*

Child: *Stays on side, agitated.*

When the child gets up and moves through the room, the adult follows.

Adult: *Moves to side of child. Places puzzle piece on top of own head, sneezes dramatically and allows piece to drop off.*

Child: *Gets up and walks over to toy shelf.*

The child stops moving but the adult continues to follow the child's lead by following his eye gaze, making a game out of what the child is looking at.

Adult: *Quickly walks over, watching child's eye gaze.* Want?

Child: *Eye gaze toward top shelf. No eye contact with adult.*

Adult: *Takes a spinning top off top shelf.* Want?

Child: *Reaches toward train.*

Adult: Train! *Adult places child's hand on train with his and leads the child to the carpet area.*

The adult keeps her hands on the child's object of desire so that the child's attention remains on her as she works the object intermittently into the giggle game.

Child: *Comes with adult, intently watching train.*

Adult: *Lays child on back, leaning over child. Holds train up high above child's head.* Train!

Child: *Eye contact with train.*

Adult: *Softly says* Choo…choo…choo…choo… *very slowly, moving train in a zigzag pattern* (cue).

Child: *Anticipation, eye contact with adult.*

The adult provides the cue by moving the object at various heights and angles, building anticipation.

Adult: *Quickly moves train down on to child's stomach, gently tickling the child, while saying* Choo, choo *very fast and loud* (reinforcer).

Child: *Laughs.*

Repeat choo-choo train sequence for ten minutes to increase staying power.

Through experimentation, the adult finds that moving the object suddenly creates a startled response that is highly pleasurable to the child and becomes the reinforcer.

WHAT? WHEN? WHY?

Answers to common questions

Q. Do you follow the lead of the child all day?

A. No, only throughout each ten-minute giggle session. The remainder of the day is teacher directed. During opening songs, art, fine and gross motor activities, readiness skills, story time, quiet time, and community training the child follows the lead of the teacher.

Q. Does the child have difficulty following an adult's lead in other activities once giggle time is over?

A. Actually, the opposite is true. After following the lead of the child, the child is more cooperative and willing to engage in adult-directed activities. As progress is made in the giggle time sessions, significant changes are observed in other classroom activities as well.

Q. What if the child changes the turn-taking game after it has been established and played many times?

A. After a game has been established, the child may begin to elaborate and vary it for the sheer joy and creativity of it. This is a common occurrence in children without developmental language delays. They often vary a turn taking numerous times. It is important to follow the child's lead and accept his new turns, incorporating them into the established routine.

OBJECTIVES WORKSHEET

Work through resistive behaviors during interaction attempts by following lead

CHILD'S NAME_____

CURRENT LEVEL

This child exhibits a strong reaction to any intrusion. He prefers to engage himself in isolated movements and manipulation of objects. Attempts to interact with him are met with physical and verbal extremes specifically aimed at keeping others at a distance.

Date initiated_____ Date mastered_____

1. Child will allow adult to enter personal space and follow his lead without resistance or tantrum behavior for five minutes.

Date initiated_____ Date mastered_____

2. Child will allow adult to enter personal space and follow his lead without resistance or tantrum behavior for ten minutes.

It is almost as if a tune knows instinctively where it is going, even if you don't: an excellent idea in all those dreadful times when we feel so utterly stranded, lost at sea, with a non-responding autistic child. The flow of the music simply takes singer and listener along, like water down its riverbed.

Sibylle Janert, *Reaching the Young Autistic Child*

USING RHYME

KEY POINTS

Won't stay? Sing a tune, chant a chant

> *A rhyme incorporated into a giggle game provides additional auditory cues to the child, aiding their understanding that a predictable turn-taking sequence is emerging.*

> *Break the rhyme or song into short phrases and spread them throughout the joint action routine.*

> *Pair different parts of a phrase with specific movements, the cue and the reinforcing turn.*

A song or rhyme that is broken into phrases throughout a turn-taking routine can become another avenue for establishing adequate staying power. When incorporated into a turn-taking sequence, it offers the child auditory cues. When specific lines of the rhyme are paired with particular movements, such as the cue and reinforcer, the sequence of the turn taking will become clearer and predictable to the child. Pairing lines of the rhyme in these ways provides additional information as to whose turn it is, when the child's turn is near, when the cue is coming and when the routine is ending.

The adult can make up a chant as the routine develops, inserting words to suit the game or use established rhymes and songs that are short and catchy. It doesn't matter if the rhyme matches the movements of the game or if it makes sense. What does matter is developing an interaction by playing with the melodic sounds of language while attending to bouncy rhythms.

When there is a lull in the development of a giggle time routine, the short phrase of a rhyme or song can fill in the empty spaces, providing a framework for the individual communicative turns to slip into.

LET'S IMAGINE

The same rhyme with three children and three different outcomes

EXAMPLE OF FIRST CHILD

The following is the first of three examples demonstrating how the Humpty Dumpty rhyme can be used with three children. Each time it is used with a different child, the giggle game built around the rhyme will look entirely different. The outcome varies since each child is at a different communicative level. Each child contributes a different 50 percent to the development of a routine with the adult. So, each time the same rhyme is used with a different child, the look of the routine changes since each particular child's turns are unique.

PROBLEM

Nathan has very little staying power and minimal eye contact. His social smile is emerging. He enjoys rough and tumble play. He appears to have a hypo-responsive vestibular system, needing more sensation. He craves movement and enjoys being upside down.

SOLUTION

Keep the giggle game short. Nathan is familiar with the Humpty Dumpty rhyme since it is shown daily on a classroom video. Develop a short routine around this familiar rhyme. This can be accomplished by using only two lines of the Humpty Dumpty rhyme instead of its entirety. The two lines should be paired with all of the adult turns in the giggle game sequence. This will shorten the duration of the game and the wait time for the child to experience the reinforcing turn. The child's turns can be eye contact and a social smile in between the adult's phrases since they are emerging pragmatic skills, but weak. Vestibular movement should be added to maintain interest.

HUMPTY DUMPTY – EXAMPLE 1

Child: *The child is on lap, facing adult who is on a chair, and gives a sideward glance.*

Adult: *Holds trunk of child and bounces legs up and down to beat of phrase.* Humpty Dumpty sat on a wall, Humpty Dumpty…

> To increase staying power in each Humpty Dumpty example, the adult taps out the syllables of the Humpty Dumpty rhyme through a bouncing movement.

> A child will pick up the rhythm of a rhyme and may move to the beat for one of his turns.

Child: *Begins to move body side to side.*

Adult: *Continues holding trunk of child and moves child slowly side to side four times off center of lap, accenting each word of phrase with sudden exaggerated movements.* Had…a…great…big… (*cue*).

Child: *Social smile.*

Adult: Fall! *Flips child in backwards somersault off lap on to feet* (*reinforcer*).

Child: *Laughs, eye contact.*

Adult: *Laughs.*

Repeat sequence for ten minutes.

LET'S IMAGINE
_____

The same rhyme with three children and three different outcomes

EXAMPLE OF SECOND CHILD

The following is the second example of how the same rhyme, Humpty Dumpty, may look different with another child.

PROBLEM

Vito has gravitational insecurity. He is hypersensitive to motion. He is resistive when met with vestibular movement. Emergence of vocalizations/babbling is occurring.

SOLUTION

Pair very gentle movements with the Humpty Dumpty rhyme that he loves. Any sound that happens to be babbled may be accepted for one or more of his turns. Play the game on the floor, keeping his feet on the ground for security.

HUMPTY DUMPTY – EXAMPLE 2

Child: *Adult sitting on mat, legs stretched out. Child sits on knees of adult, face to face. Adult holds child's upper torso. Child gives eye contact.*

> The Humpty Dumpty giggle game is different for each child since they are at different communication levels and possess differing sensory needs. Each child contributes a different 50 percent to the development of the routine.

Adult: *Adult covers child's head with scarf.* Humpty Dumpty sat on a wall, Humpty Dumpty... *Bounces very slowly and lightly and then waits expectantly.*

Child: *Continues gentle up and down movement of the game.*

Adult: had...a...great...BIG... *Lifts edge of scarf up and down and suddenly stops the bouncing movement (cue).*

Child: Ah.

Adult: FALL! *Drops child softly between legs on to the mat, quickly removing the scarf at the same time (reinforcer).*

Child: *Social smile.*

Repeat sequence for ten minutes.

LET'S IMAGINE

The same rhyme with three children and three different outcomes

EXAMPLE OF THIRD CHILD

This is the third example of how the same rhyme appears different with each child.

PROBLEM

Sammy craves joint compression and deep pressure. He actively seeks out large pieces of equipment that he can wedge himself between. He often rams into other children and adults. One might describe him as a "hectic" child. He is beginning to use word approximations.

SOLUTION

Utilize a large prop that provides resistance and that the child can move into during a portion of the game. Pushing him into the prop provides needed input into the joints and muscles (*a "rough and tumble" reinforcer offering deep pressure may prove to be effective*).

HUMPTY DUMPTY – EXAMPLE 3

> Since each child depicted in the Humpty Dumpty examples lacks staying power, only the first two lines of the rhyme are used throughout the giggle games.

Child: *Adult helps child sit on top of large sensory ball and holds child's torso. Ball is anchored up against another object to keep it from rolling and is on a mat.*

Adult: *Quickly bounces child up and down on top of ball.* Humpty Dumpty sat on a wall, Humpty Dumpty...

Child: *Eye contact, social smile.*

Adult: had...a...great...big... *Bounces child slowly, accenting each word with a bounce* (cue).

Child: Faw.

Adult: FALL! *Suddenly slides child off ball on to the mat and squeezes him, flipping him from side to side on the mat* (reinforcer).

Child: *Laughs.*

Adult: More? More?

Child: Mo.

Repeat sequence for ten minutes.

Humpty Dumpty (I)

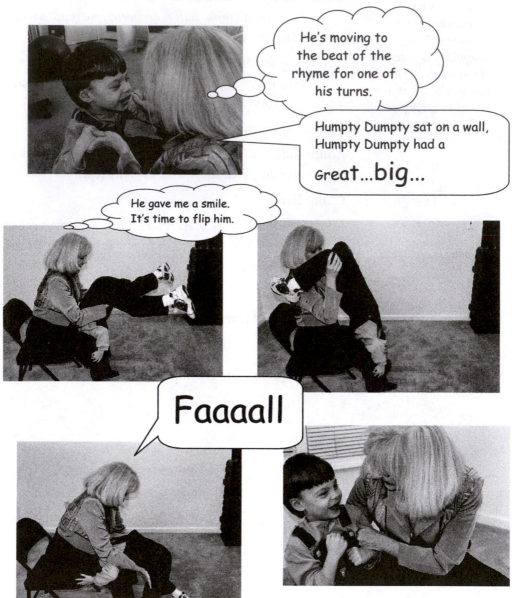

This child has little staying power, yet enjoys rough and tumble play. Bouncing the child to the beat of "Humpty Dumpty" as well as flipping him sustains his proximity.

Humpty Dumpty (2)

> Humpy Dumpty sat on a wall, Humpy Dumpty had a
>
> Great big...

> She's stopped talking and bouncing, it must be my turn.

> Ah

The adult's cessation of a rhythmic movement to a rhyme is a stimulus for creating a turn from this child.

> Faaaaaaaaall!

This child has gravitational insecurity and is hypersensitive to movement. The soft, gentle, rhythmic movement of this Humpty Dumpty giggle game is played close to the floor on the adult's knees. The cue is the cessation of movement and sound. The reinforcing turn is a sudden removal of the scarf and a gentle 3–4 inch drop from the adult's legs to the floor. The removal of the scarf adds an element of surprise.

Humpty Dumpty (3)

Since this child craves deep pressure, a large ball is incorporated into the Humpty Dumpty rhyme. Resistance is provided when he is bounced firmly into it.

EXAMPLES: ESTABLISHED RHYMES

(Adapted from *Baby Games* (E. Martin 1988, Running Press Publishers))

Established traditional rhymes can aid the development of adult turns in giggle time routines. In these examples, the adult's actions that correlate with each phrase have been left blank since they are unique to the two personalities involved. The adult's actions depend on the likes and dislikes of the child. The child's response has been left blank, as it will depend on his current communicative level. Possible cues and reinforcing lines have been suggested. Remember, if the child's staying power is weak, use only several adult lines of the rhyme and then repeat.

ONE FOR THE MONEY

> Adult: One for the money,
>
> Child:
>
> Adult: Two for the show,
>
> Child:
>
> Adult: Three to get ready,
>
> Child:
>
> Adult: And four…to… (*cue*)
>
> Child:
>
> Adult: go! (*Pair this word with reinforcer.*)
>
> Child:
>
> (Traditional, Great Britain, United States)

Sequence is repeated for ten minutes.

OH, MR SUN

> Adult: Oh, Mr Sun Sun, Mr Golden Sun
>
> Child:
>
> Adult: Please shine down on me.
>
> Child:
>
> Adult: Oh, Mr Sun Sun, Mr Golden Sun

Child:

Adult: Hiding behind the tree.

Child:

Adult: These little children are asking you

Child:

Adult: to please come out so we can play with you.

Child:

Adult: Oh, Mr Sun…Sun…Mr…Golden…Sun, (*cue*)

Child:

Adult: Please shine down on, please shine down on, please shine down on me! (*Pair this line with reinforcer.*)

Child:

(Traditional, Southern United States)

Repeat sequence for ten minutes.

BOOM, BANG, BOOM, BANG!

Adult: Boom, bang, boom, bang!

Child:

Adult: Rumpety, lumpety, bump!

Child:

Adult: Zoom, zam, zoom, zam!

Child:

Adult: Clippety, clappety, clump! (*cue*)

Child:

Adult: What wonderful noises a thunderstorm brings! (*Pair this line with reinforcer.*)

Child:

(Traditional, North America)

Repeat sequence for ten minutes.

THE GRAND OLD DUKE OF YORK

Adult: Oh the Grand Old Duke of York, he had ten thousand men.

Child:

Adult: He led them up to the top of the hill

Child:

Adult: and he led them down again.

Child:

Adult: And when they were up they were up.

Child:

Adult: And when they were down they were down.

Child:

Adult: And when they were only half way up (*cue*)

Child:

Adult: They were neither up nor down! (*Pair this line with reinforcer.*)

Child:

(Traditional, England)

Sequence is repeated for ten minutes.

ALPHABET SONG

Adult: A B C D E F G

Child:

Adult: H I J K L M N O P

Child:

Adult: Q R S T U V

Child:

Adult: W...X...Y... (*cue*)

Child:

Adult: Z! Now I know my ABCs next time won't you sing with me? (*Pair this line with reinforcer.*)

Child:

(Traditional, North America)

Sequence is repeated for ten minutes.

ONE TWO BUCKLE MY SHOE

Adult: One two buckle my shoe.

Child:

Adult: Three four shut the door.

Child:

Adult: Five six pick up sticks.

Child:

Adult: Seven eight lay them straight.

Child:

Adult: Nine…ten… (*cue*)

Child:

Adult: a big fat hen! (*Pair this line with reinforcer.*)

Child:

(Traditional, England)

Repeat sequence for ten minutes

RING AROUND THE ROSY

Adult: Ring around the rosy

Child:

Adult: a pocket full of posies,

Child:

Adult: Ashes, ashes

Child:

Adult: We all…fall… (*cue*)

Child:

Adult: down! (*Pair this word with reinforcer.*)

Child:

(Traditional, Great Britain, North America)

Sequence is repeated for ten minutes.

TROT, TROT, TROT

Adult: Trot, trot, trot to London.

Child:

Adult: Trot, trot, trot to Denver.

Child:

Adult: Look...out...[*child's name*]... (*cue*)

Child:

Adult: or you might fall over! (*Pair this line with reinforcer.*)

Child:

(Traditional, England)

Sequence is repeated for ten minutes.

ROW, ROW, ROW THE BOAT

Adult: Row, row, row the boat

Child:

Adult: gently down the stream.

Child:

Adult: Merrily, merrily, merrily, merrily

Child:

Adult: life...is...but...a... (*cue*)

Child:

Adult: dream! (*Pair this line with reinforcer.*)

Child:

(Traditional, Great Britain, North America)

Repeat sequence for ten minutes.

THIS IS THE WAY THE LADIES RIDE

Adult: This is the way the ladies ride, the ladies ride, the ladies ride.

Child:

Adult: This is the way the ladies ride, so early in the morning.

Child:

Adult: This is the way the gentleman rides, the gentleman rides, the gentleman rides.

Child:

Adult: this is the way the gentleman rides, so early in the morning.

Child:

Adult: A...n...d... (*cue*)

Child:

Adult: this is the way the farmer rides, the farmer rides, the farmer rides. This is the way the farmer rides, so early in the morning. (*Pair this line with reinforcer.*)

Child:

(Traditional, Great Britain, adapted)

Sequence is repeated for ten minutes.

JACK IN THE BOX

Adult: Jack in the box

Child.

Adult sits so still.

Child:

Adult: Won't you come out? (*cue*)

Child:

Adult: Yes! I will! (*Pair this line with reinforcer.*)

Child:

(Traditional, United States)

Repeat sequence for ten minutes.

JACK 'N JILL

Adult: Jack 'n Jill went up the hill

Child:

Adult: to fetch a pail of water.

Child:

Adult: Jack fell down

Child:

Adult: and broke his crown (*cue*)

Child:

Adult: and Jill came tumbling after. (*Pair this line with reinforcer.*)

Child:

(Traditional, England, Medieval Norse)

Sequence is repeated for ten minutes.

FEE FIE FOE FUM

Adult: Fee Fie Foe Fum.

Child:

Adult: Big giant here I come.

Child:

Adult: Fee Fie foe fum. (*cue*)

Child:

Adult: Watch out, here I come! (*Pair this line with reinforcer.*)

Child:

(Traditional, Great Britain)

Repeat sequence for ten minutes.

TEDDY BEAR

Adult: Round like a circle

Child:

Adult: like a teddy bear.

Child:

Adult: One step…two steps… (*cue*)

Child:

Adult: tickle under there! (*Pair this line with reinforcer.*)

(Traditional, England, adapted)

Repeat sequence for ten minutes.

ALL AROUND THE COBBLER'S BENCH

Adult: All around the cobbler's bench

Child:

Adult: the monkey chased the weasel.

Child:

Adult: The monkey thought it was all...in...fun... (*cue*)

Child:

Adult: Pop! Goes the weasel! (*Pair this line with reinforcer.*)

(Traditional, United States, adapted)

Repeat sequence for ten minutes.

HIGGLETY, PIGGLETY, POP

Adult: Higglety, pigglety, pop.

Child:

Adult: The dog has eaten the mop.

Child:

Adult: The pig's in a hurry, the cat's in a flurry.

Child:

Adult: Higglety...pigglety... (*cue*)

Child:

Adult: pop! (*Pair this line with reinforcer.*)

(Samuel Griswold Goodrich, United States, 1846)

Repeat sequence for ten minutes.

ENGINE ENGINE

Adult: Engine engine number nine

Child:

Adult: coming down [*child's name*] line.

Child:

Adult: If the train goes off the track,

Child:

Adult: do you want your money back?

Child:

Adult: Yes…no… (*cue*)

Child:

Adult: maybe so! (*Pair this line with reinforcer.*)

Child:

(Traditional, Great Britain, North America)

Repeat sequence for ten minutes.

DID YOU EVER SEE A LASSIE?

Adult: Did you ever see a lassie, a lassie, a lassie?

Child:

Adult: Did you ever see a lassie…go… (*cue*)

Child:

Adult: this way and that! (*Pair this line with reinforcer.*)

Child:

(Traditional, Great Britain, North America)

Repeat sequence for ten minutes.

WHAT? WHEN? WHY?

Answers to common questions

Q. Why is the rhyme, chant or song kept short?

A. The child's staying power may be short and he may be unable to tolerate a long rhyme. The child would have to wait too long for his turn. If staying power is weak, the entire routine shouldn't be any longer than four turns, including the cue and reinforcing turn – two turns for the adult and two turns for the child.

Q. Why do the phrases of the rhyme need to be paired with movement?

A. This increases the likelihood of staying power. The movement is paired with the beat of the rhyme, song or chant.

Q. How do I know which line to cue and which line to use as the reinforcer?

A. They are always toward the end of the routine. The last line of the rhyme can be broken down into both the cue and the reinforcer. The cue can accompany the beginning of the last line and the reinforcer can accompany the last word. Or the last two lines of the rhyme can be reserved for the cue and reinforcer.

Q. What if I use a rhyme or song and begin to lose the interest of the child?

A. Perhaps the phrases of the song are too long. Shorten them even more and add an accompanying movement that the child enjoys. It is not necessary to complete a rhyme or song in its entirety. One or two lines stretched throughout the routine are enough to serve the purpose.

Q. What if the child doesn't appear interested in the rhymes that I use?

A. Choose rhymes or songs from favorite videos, musical tapes, or favorite books that he has repetitive exposure to and enjoys.

Q. What if the child appears to enjoy the routine while engaged, but wants to leave right after the first sequence? Do I follow his lead and drop the successful routine?

A. You may have to follow his lead and change the game but since he appeared to enjoy it, try this first. Immediately after the sequence ends, begin again. Do not hesitate more than one second between repetitions. If you hesitate longer than that, you will give the child an opportunity to escape. Keep the routine moving at a very fast pace.

OBJECTIVES WORKSHEET

Remain engaged in a giggle game when a song, rhyme, or chant is used

CHILD'S NAME_____

CURRENT LEVEL

This child may lack obvious affect in facial expression, making it difficult to tell if he is enjoying a giggle game. He may even leave the area if there is a momentary lull. He does not yet signal the adult to continue a game through gesture, vocalization or body movement.

Date initiated_____ Date mastered_____

1. Given an interaction involving a favorite song, rhyme or chant, the child will display pleasure through one or more of the following: social smile, laughter or heightened affect.

Date initiated_____ Date mastered_____

2. When a phrase of a song, rhyme or chant is momentarily stopped, the child will continue the giggle game by making a movement of the game or by touching the adult. (Adult shapes the movement or touch to be a meaningful turn in the game by quickly responding to it with an interesting adult turn.)

Date initiated_____ Date mastered_____

3. When a phrase of a song, rhyme or chant is momentarily stopped before the reinforcing turn, the child will continue the giggle game by vocalizing a word approximation of the reinforcing turn, signaling the adult to continue.

Life is ebb and flow, peaks and valleys, struggles and sweet times.
What we fail to realize, all too often, is that the struggles make
possible the times that are sweet.

Karen Casey, *Each Day a New Beginning*

USING MOVEMENT

KEY POINTS

Not staying? Keep moving

> One way to increase staying power is through vestibular movements.

As an assortment of joint action routines are created, communication skills are strengthened and the child's staying power naturally increases. The child begins to feel the joy associated with communicating in a joint action routine and remains for a longer time. However, keeping the child within proximity long enough to develop these routines can be a challenge. One way that the adult can encourage staying power as a routine develops is through vestibular movement. The vestibular system detects movement and responses to gravity from its receptors in the inner ear. There are five different vestibular movements that can be incorporated into joint action routines. They are sagittal (side to side), frontal (back and forth), transverse (around), orbital (linear and transverse combined) and linear (forward).

> The lower the level of staying power, the more vestibular movement is needed.

For example, moving a child side to side on top of a bolster is an example of sagittal movement. Incorporating a rocking motion into a routine is an example of a frontal movement. Twirling a child around in a circle is an example of a transverse movement. Pushing and twirling a child in a rolling chair is an example of an orbital movement. Pushing the child across the room on a tricycle and suddenly stopping is an example of a linear movement. These vestibular movements are large muscle, or gross motor, movement. The lower the level

Whenever a movement is incorporated into a routine, it should be paired with a sound, word or phrase.

The movement should not be any longer than the sound, word or phrase that accompanies it.

of staying power, the greater the need for movement to maintain interest.

Many children crave vestibular movement and the insertion of these movements into routines significantly lengthens their staying power. Swinging, rowing, twirling, pulling, and flipping can be reinforcers in the turn-taking sequence for these children. Others, however, are hypersensitive to vestibular movements. In these cases, movements are incorporated as tolerated and in a gentle, slow, methodical manner. Vestibular movement needs to be monitored carefully for side-effects. Occupational therapists are your greatest resource for determining the levels of vestibular stimulation appropriate for any given child.

Research indicates that vestibular movements aid not only in the development of spatial perception, expressive and receptive language, attention, memory, emotion and nonverbal cues, but in the normalization of all the sensory systems, including tactile (Jensen 1998). The child's tactile system plays a key role in the development of adequate staying power.

There are two parts of the tactile system, the protective and the discriminative systems (Kranowitz 1998). Both are apparent at birth. The discriminative system provides information of what is touching the child, the location of the touch and whether the touch is light or deep. This system calms and organizes. The protective system alerts him to danger and instills the need for fight or flight. If this system is receiving inaccurate information, friendly, casual contact triggers extreme reactions. The child may have great difficulty in allowing another in his personal space and in tolerating light touch. He may not feel safe when others are near. In normal development, this system matures as the child ages and accurate information regarding safety is received. However, some children have come under my care with this part of the tactile system still alerting

Rather than thinking of the child as rejecting you, think of the child as uncomfortable in the situation.

them to continual danger. By slowly incorporating movement into giggle time routines, I have noted that children's tactile defensiveness gradually becomes less pronounced and they begin to allow closer proximity and touch in the routines.

It can be uncomfortable to continually pursue a child that turns away and shrieks in dismay. It takes courage to endure the sharp pain of rejection day after day. However, each time interaction is attempted with movement, the likelihood of lengthening the child's staying period increases. As it increases, the child's eye contact, their gentle touch, and the musical sound of their laughter will begin to connect you to him. Embrace these moments, for as quickly as they come, just as abruptly they will leave. The next time interaction is attempted, the child may once again be slow to respond. The closeness and communication that was previously attained may feel lost. However, persevere and remain confident that the intensity and staying power of the previous turn taking will eventually return and be sweeter than the last.

LET'S IMAGINE

How to incorporate movement to increase staying power

EXAMPLE

In the following example, staying power is increased through the addition of a transverse vestibular movement.

PROBLEM

Giovanni is nonverbal. His staying power is weak. When his personal space is invaded, he swiftly runs away. Eye contact is fleeting.

SOLUTION

Incorporate his movement of running away as one of his turns in a giggle game sequence. When eye gaze is received, react quickly with an adult turn to reinforce it.

DOG

The adult adds short words to short spurts of movement.	Child: *Running around room.* Adult: *Crawls slowly toward child, with each crawling movement makes one long barking sound.*
The adult adds one elongated word to slow exaggerated movements.	Adult: *Jumps up and moves quickly toward child, making many "arf" sounds.* Child: *Eye contact, runs.* Adult: *Nuzzles child's socks and legs of pants while growling (cue).*
The pace of the adult's movement is paired with the pace of the adult's vocalizations. When the adult is moving slowly, she talks slowly. When the adult is moving quickly, her speech matches the pace.	Child: *Smiles.* Adult: *Jumps up and holds child under arms and twirls around one time.* Doggie's going to get you! (*Reinforcer.*) Child: *Laughs.* **Repeat sequence for ten minutes.**

Dog

Running away can be a child's turn.

The adult moves from a crawling position to an upright position. Changing planes of body positioning heightens the excitement.

The adult provides the child with a cue by growling and nuzzling the leg of his pants.

WHAT? WHEN? WHY?

Answers to common questions

Q. Why do you pair a movement with a sound, word or phrase?

A. A sound, word or phrase by itself does not create the same interest. Paired with movement, the turn offers more cues to the child. If the child does not attend to the sound, word or phrase, he may attend to the movement. With pairing, the adult's turn becomes memorable and predictable.

Q. You spoke of initially creating a small play space of six inches to one foot. How can movement be incorporated into a small area?

A. In order to promote staying power, some children initially need a turn-taking play space of six inches to one foot. Sitting on the floor, holding hands and rowing back and forth would be an example of incorporating movement into a small play space. Also, facing the child toward you on your lap, as the child is bounced, flipped and moved from side to side or up and down, would be another example of incorporating movement into a small play space.

Q. What are the other children doing as I attempt to increase the staying power of one?

A. They are engaged in free play activities or similarly engaged with another adult. As the turn-taking builds, the energy and excitement associated with the routine becomes contagious and other children often establish proximity. If the sequence has been repetitively played and is firmly established, the adult may be able to incorporate another child into the routine. Each time the reinforcer is played, the adult may be able to play that turn with each child within proximity. This also encourages staying power as the original child waits for a few seconds. However, if more than one turn is played with the new player, you may lose the staying power of the original child.

OBJECTIVES WORKSHEET

Increase staying power when movement is incorporated into giggle games

CHILD'S NAME _____

CURRENT LEVEL

This child may resist movement. Experimenting with various types of movements and pace may prove to be helpful. Or, he may enjoy vestibular movements throughout other parts of the day but still lack the staying power to successfully remain engaged in giggle games. The addition of his favored movements into his games may substantially increase his staying power so that other communicative skills may be learned.

Date initiated_____ Date mastered_____

1. Given a giggle game routine involving vestibular motion, the student will tolerate the movement and remain in proximity of the partner.

Date initiated_____ Date mastered_____

2. Given a giggle game routine involving vestibular motion, the student will attend to the adult by engaging in a series of turns for ten minutes.

To share your life with a child is to humble yourself so that you may learn from them and discover with them the beautiful secrets that are only uncovered in searching.

Kathleen Tierney Crilly, *Each Day a New Beginning*

USING IMITATION

KEY POINTS

When all else fails, imitate

Turn taking in an imitative sequence is often without language. Sounds and movements are the norm.

If you feel that you are continually losing the child's interest and staying power you may be at a communicative level that is too high for the child. Try imitation. When you imitate the child, you communicate at their level and they remain in the interaction for a longer time period.

During imitation, you are at the child's communicative level and staying power increases.

By imitating, you are doing both something the child can do, as well as something he wants to do. An imitation is like a compliment. When you act like the child, you show that you accept him. The child will often pay more attention and remain in the interaction longer. (MacDonald 1989)

Imitative turn taking is pre-conversational. Each partner is waiting for the other to complete his or her turn.

As the child is imitated, he will begin to watch very carefully, making sure that his actions and sounds are being followed. This gives the child an enhanced opportunity to observe his own actions and the results of those actions on people and objects. It places the child in control of the environment and the adult's performance. This in turn reinforces the child's initiations (Tiegerman and Primavera 1981).

In the beginning, one may see only slight movements and hear soft sounds, like the slight lift of a finger or a whisper. However, the imitation of even the slightest movements and sounds appears to impact the child's feeling of control. As he becomes confident of the adult's role, his movements and vocalizations will become more conspicuous. The turn taking will gradually develop into a steady "conversational flow" of babbling, noises, vocalizations, motor movements and exaggerated facial expressions.

There are, however, several key elements needed for successful imitation. During imitation, the adult's turns should be no longer than the child's. Also, it is important to wait "expectantly" after each imitation. As you wait and watch in anticipation, you will almost see the "wheels turning" as he creates his next turn. Also, the adult must be agile and willing to move around the room. It is not unusual to find an imitating adult following a child under tables, through tiny boxes, over toys and jumping across the room! The play space must be as small as possible, keeping the distance between the adult and child within two feet. Imitate in front of the child when possible, moving to the side when active movement is involved. If you find yourself trailing behind, make it obvious that you are there. Exaggerated footsteps, the tapping of objects, or the possession of a noisemaker will increase the child's awareness of your presence.

Keeping the play space small is imperative for successful imitation.

Last, be prepared for unexpected visitors. These invariably arrive during imitative sessions which may look quite odd to a spectator. However, the excitement and enthusiasm of finally making a connection with the child will overplay any embarrassment. The spectator will also be in awe as they observe an increase in the child's communicative turn taking, eye contact, social smile and length of staying power.

One can't give a child what they don't possess. If the child is to become more animated and playful, then the adult must be more animated and playful.

Sometimes it is necessary to alter your behavior to make a difference with a particular child. Imitation is a training ground where you can acquire new skills and practice a different approach. Until the choice is made to act differently, you may continue to get the same results that you got yesterday, last week or last month. Bringing

Become the child's mirror for ten minutes.

All facial expressions, sounds, vocalizations and small and large motor movements must be imitated precisely.

out the playful child within you may be just what makes the difference. Imitation will provide you with an opportunity to stretch and move beyond what is comfortable. Even though self-consciousness may accompany your initial attempts, persevere and this serious exterior will be shed and you will become more animated in sound and movement. You will become visually and auditorily stimulating, which will enable you to become more desirable to the child than the distractions around him. As you practice imitation, you will discover that the child is teaching you as well. You will learn how to live in the present moment as you carefully imitate second to second. Also, you will uncover your playfulness, which has been buried under the responsibilities of daily life.

LET'S IMAGINE

How imitation of sounds and movement increases staying power

EXAMPLE

The following is an example of how to successfully imitate a child in order to increase their staying power. The child's staying power must be increased before giggle games can be developed.

PROBLEM

David resists any attempt at interaction by the arching of his back and twists of his body. He prefers tapping objects repetitively and opening and closing cupboards. If the adult persists in attempting interaction, he screams in agitation.

SOLUTION

Stay within 12 inches of the child at all times. Attempt to remain face to face and at eye level whenever possible. Become his shadow and follow his lead. Imitate all sounds and movements with precision. Don't talk.

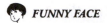 *FUNNY FACE*

Not sure what to do on your turn? Imitate all sounds and movements.	**Child:** *Sitting on floor, tapping floor with object.* **Adult:** *Finds same or similar object, crouches low in front of child to maximize eye contact, taps floor with object.* **Child:** *Stops tapping, sits very still.*
If the child has an object, retrieve a similar object and imitate all movements.	**Adult:** *Stops tapping, sits very still.* **Child:** *Resumes tapping.* **Adult:** *Waits a few seconds, resumes tapping.* **Child:** *Turns body away.* **Adult:** *Turns body away.* **Child:** *Watches out of corner of eye.* **Adult:** *Watches out of corner of eye.*
If the child gets up and moves, move alongside of him, staying within one to two feet.	**Child:** *Stands abruptly, walks to corner of room.* **Adult:** *Stands, walks closely beside child to corner of room.* **Child:** *Opens mouth wide.* **Adult:** *Opens mouth wide.*
Don't vocalize unless the child vocalizes.	**Child:** Ugh. **Adult:** Ugh. **Child:** *Gallops across room.* **Adult:** *Gallops across room, loudly.* **Child:** *Eye contact, emerging smile.*
Doing something with another person is a step up from doing something in isolation.	**Adult:** *Gives eye contact, exaggerated smile and then waits expectantly.* **Child:** *Closes eyes and opens them.* **Adult:** *Closes eyes and opens them.* **Child:** *Puckers lips together, eye contact.* **Adult:** *Puckers lips together in exaggeration, eye contact.* **Child:** *Gallops across room quickly, stops suddenly.* **Adult:** *Gallops loudly across room, stops suddenly.* **Child:** *Crawls into large box and out the other side.*

Adult: *Crawls right behind child, into box and out the other side.*

Child: *Sits on floor, raises arm.*

Adult: *Sits on floor, raises arm.*

Child: *Touches nose to adult's nose.*

Adult: *Touches nose to child's nose.*

Continue imitation for minimum of ten minutes.

Funny Face

Imitate face to face, eye level to eye level.

When the child "allows" the adult to imitate him, he has moved up a step from isolation.

Imitation becomes a giggle game that two can play.

Imitation may be subtle and localized to one area of the room, or may include gross motor movements throughout the room.

WHAT? WHEN? WHY?

Answers to common questions

Q. When the child was tapping, why did the adult wait a few seconds before tapping his object?

A. The adult needed to establish a feeling of taking turns. If the adult taps simultaneously, the child may not even be aware of the tapping.

Q. How does the adult "wait expectantly?'

A. By crouching down low near eye level, watching the child's face intently, moving the head in toward the child slightly, and raising the eyebrows. You must remain very still in that position for ten to fifteen seconds, visually cueing the child that it is their turn to "do something."

Q. When an adult imitates the child, are they reinforcing "autistic-like" behaviors?

A. One must use judgment and not imitate biting, hitting, licking, or other behaviors that are abusive to the child or another. One may, however, twirl, gallop, run, rock, hide, sway, line up or twirl objects. Once the child understands that he is being "followed," perseverance of any one movement does not occur. Many movements become incorporated into the imitation giggle game and some are quite creative as well as physically challenging! Remember that growth is accomplished in baby steps, one small step at a time. Doing something with another human being is a step up from doing something in isolation. Imitation is only a place to begin. Once rapport and staying power are established through imitation, other giggle games follow.

Q. What if it's not possible to keep the play space small?

A. It is difficult to keep the play space small when there is a lot of movement around the room. However, a small play space is imperative. If the adult is too far away, the child will not realize that his actions are impacting the adult's behavior. It must be very obvious that all movements, sounds and facial expressions are being followed for a turn taking to develop. Close proximity is necessary to see the subtle signs that the child makes as he becomes increasingly aware of the imitation. If the adult is close enough, he will see the child turn slightly or quickly dart his eyes to make sure that he is being imitated. As the child gains reassurance that he is really in control of the game, he will begin to wait for the adult to complete the imitation before engaging in his next movement. This is an indication that true turn taking and pre-conversational flow is developing.

Q.   I have been following and imitating the child around the room. He appears very interested but will not stop moving. Is there anything else that I can do to encourage staying power?

A.   Follow the child into a large, enclosed space and then block his escape route. A playhouse with a door, a large box or a tunnel is an appropriate example. This tightens up the play space and the chances of a successful interaction increase.

Q.   Why is it important to keep my turn the same length as the child's?

A.   It is important for the child to *feel* he is the lead. If the adult's turn is longer, he may become confused and feel that he is not in control of the interaction. His staying power will be lost.

OBJECTIVES WORKSHEET

Developing giggle games that involve imitation to increase staying power

CHILD'S NAME_____

CURRENT LEVEL

This child is aware of the imitation but is not yet letting it become a game that two can play. He does not yet repeat or vary his movements to see how they affect the adult. He seems uncomfortable with this close proximity and continually leaves the area.

Date initiated_____ Date mastered_____

1. Given an adult imitating the child's movements and sounds/vocalizations, the child will continue the interaction by repeating his earlier movements and vocalizations.

Date initiated_____ Date mastered_____

2. Given an adult imitating the child's movements and sounds/vocalizations, the child will continue the interaction by varying his patterns of movement and vocalizations.

Date initiated_____ Date mastered_____

3. Given an adult imitating the child, the child will continue "leading" the adult through various movements and vocalizations/sounds for ten minutes.

When we approach life tentatively, we reap only a portion of its gifts. It's like watching a movie in black and white that's supposed to be in Technicolor. Our lives are in color, but we must have courage to let the colors emerge; to feel them, absorb them and be changed by them.

Karen Casey, *Each Day a New Beginning*

USING PROPS

KEY POINTS

Playing with an object? Use it as a giggle game prop!

Shift the child's attention from the object by creating animated, exaggerated, creative movements with the object.

Strive to become more interesting than the objects surrounding the child.

The toy becomes a game prop; you become the toy.

Playing with the object in its functional way keeps the attention on the object rather than on you.

Some of these children are involved with the manipulation of objects to the exclusion of social interaction, which makes the development of a giggle time routine difficult to attain. In order to be successful, the child's attention must shift from the object to the adult. Becoming the object of interest will shift this attention. The adult must become the toy: a silly, animated, playful, creative toy! How does one do this? The term "make it bigger" describes the exaggeration and drama that is necessary while interacting with these youngsters (Janert 2000). By responding in a "bigger" way, the adult can become more interesting than the child's object of desire. As she becomes more interesting, the child's attention shifts from the object to the developing turn taking. James MacDonald (1998) states that people are the toys a child needs in order to learn how to communicate. As you work on becoming the child's toy, the object is incorporated into the turn-taking routine. It is incorporated for three reasons. First, the child is interested in it; second, you are following the child's lead; and, third, it will increase staying power when it is in the child's visual field. The way it is incorporated is by using it as a giggle game prop. However, as the object is incorporated, it should

Using an object that the child enjoys increases staying power in a turn-taking routine.

not be used for its intended purpose. When it is used in the conventional way, the focused attention continues to be on it instead of on the adult. The adult must invent new functions for the object.

As the adult creates new twists and turns with the object, the child's curiosity and interest will be stimulated. When this happens, the child's staying power will increase and the building of a joint action routine quickly follows.

LET'S IMAGINE

How to incorporate the child's desired object into a giggle game

EXAMPLE

In the following example, the child's interest in an object is used as a vehicle to encourage joint attention and social reciprocity.

PROBLEM

Adam is passive and nonverbal. He does not engage in appropriate action with objects. When approached, he quickly moves away. Eye contact is fleeting. He is often engaged in the flipping of objects while lying on his back, desiring visual stimulation.

SOLUTION

Incorporate Adam's preferred body position into a giggle game, having him lying on his back as one of his turns. Use the object as a prop that you both can manipulate. Take his fleeting eye contact and his proximity as possible turns. As you become more interesting than the object through your animated, exaggerated movements, you will set up the positive pairing of you with the object. This will increase the likelihood of further interaction with you in the future. Move the object at various heights and pace for visual attention.

LAUNDRY BASKET

Child: *Lying on his back, twirling a laundry basket above his head.*

The adult shifts the child's interest from the object to the adult by doing something silly with the object.

Adult: *Stands over child, placing feet on either side of child's body. She bends over child and holds on to the basket, quickly lifting it high over her own head.* Up. *Quickly places it back down into child's hands.* Down.

Child: *Eye contact, interest. The adult should begin to formulate the cue and reinforcing turn now.*

When the adult does not receive interest after manipulating the child's object in a silly manner, she alters her turn, trying another silly manipulation.

Adult: *Using the same body posture, slowly lifts the basket off the child's head.* U…p. *Speaks slowly and uses a soft voice inflection of low to high to dignify the cue. Places it high above her own head (cue).*

Child: *Eye contact, interest, joint attention on object, reaches up toward object.*

Adult: *Quickly places the basket straight down on to the child's head.*

Child: *Eye contact, social smile.*

Adult: *Tickles.*

Child: *Turns body away. (Alter.)*

Adult: *Gently shakes the child's body back and forth.* Down, down, down! *(Reinforcer.)*

Child: *Laughs.*

Repeat sequence for ten minutes, omitting altered adult turn.

Laundry Basket

This child enjoys lying on his back and flipping objects. Incorporate these body movements into a giggle game and use the object as a prop that both can manipulate.

Become more interesting than the object with animated, exaggerated movements.

By manipulating the object around the adult and child's body, attention is drawn away from the object and is moved towards the adult.

The child's arm movement towards the basket is one of his turns.

A positive pairing of the object with a social interaction has occurred.

WHAT? WHEN? WHY?

Answers to common questions

Q. What if I don't have any ideas of how to begin a giggle session around a child's play with an object?

A. Jump right in. You will immediately begin to feel light-hearted as you experiment with silly, playful movements. Remember to use the object in dramatic, exaggerated ways.

Q. Why can't I use the object for its intended purpose?

A. The child's attention will remain focused on the object instead of on you. You must bring the attention to you. You can do this by manipulating the object around your own body. Bounce it off your head, hide it behind you, throw it high and then fall over dramatically.

Q. After reading the previous example, I wondered if you would bring out the laundry basket the next day to play the same giggle game?

A. Yes, especially if the child is difficult to reach and I don't have a repertoire of other giggle games established with him. I might place the basket in the toy area and wait for the child to establish proximity to it, watching for eye gaze toward me. I would then say "Play? Basket?" and begin the routine. This would reinforce the child's proximity to the object and eye gaze toward me, shaping further nonverbal communicative behaviors. It would also be the beginning stages of shaping the child's initiation of routines. Another technique, which is explained in detail in a later chapter, involves one member of staff manipulating the child's hands to hold on to the basket while bringing it to another staff member. The member of staff who is prompting the child helps him place it in the second staff member's hands. Then the game begins. However, one must not make the walk from one staff member to another very far since initiation of a routine is being trained with this procedure and the child may not understand why he is being moved. The result may be tantrum behavior.

Q. What if the child is only interested in crayons and paper, a doll, a puzzle piece, sticky notepaper, letters or numbers?

A. The same rules apply. Observe the child and find out what object he loves. Then use that object as a prop in the turn-taking routines. If the child loves letters, your game should include the alphabet. Sticky notepaper? Stick it on his head, your nose, his knee, and so on. Is he involved with crayons and paper? Get your own crayon and paper, imitate and then intersperse silly turns into the routine. Favorite doll or puzzle piece? Begin with imitation and then incorporate creative turns that move the child's eye contact to you. This will take time so do not give up. The child within you is waiting and willing to rise to this occasion.

OBJECTIVES WORKSHEET

Develop giggle games around favored objects to increase staying power

CHILD'S NAME_____

CURRENT LEVEL

This child is often found twirling, piling, holding or flipping an object/objects in isolation. He may shriek or quickly turn away when an adult intrudes upon him and the object.

Date initiated_____ Date mastered_____

1. Given a child involved with an object, the child will allow the adult to establish close proximity and briefly manipulate the object.

Date initiated_____ Date mastered_____

2. Given a child with an object, the child will develop with the adult a turn-taking sequence involving the object.

Date initiated_____ Date mastered_____

3. Once a giggle time routine involving an object is momentarily stopped, the child will continue the interaction by using one or more of the following: eye contact, touching adult, social smile or vocalization.

A woman is meant to hold the heart of the world in her hands. She must cater to it and minister to it and kiss it when it cries. We are meant to keep the home fires burning, the fires in our hearts. We are meant to prepare the food, the spiritual food of love and compassion. We are meant to care for the children, not just our own, but every child.

Marianne Williamson, *A Womans Worth*

SETTING THE PACE

KEY POINTS

Still not staying? Shorten it and pick up the pace

Shorten the routine but lengthen the reinforcing turn.

When quickening the pace of a routine, the adult should only take two turns, the cue and reinforcing turn.

When staying power is weak, the entire giggle game sequence must not be any longer than four turns and 15 to 20 seconds in duration.

No more than two seconds should elapse between ending the routine and beginning it again.

There will be children who, despite following lead, rhymes, movement, imitation and object play, refuse to stay with you. These children exhibit an extreme lack of "staying power." It is very difficult not to take their rejection personally since their lack of interest and fleeting appearance are obvious not only to you but to everyone around you as well. However, don't give up. There is one way in. The length of the joint action routine must be very *short* and the pace must be very *fast.*

The total length of the routine should not be any longer than four turns; two turns for you and two for the child. Your turns are simply the cue and reinforcing turn. The cue should consist of a sound or single word paired with movement. The reinforcing turn should consist of one word or a short phrase paired with movement and an element of surprise. The child's two turns might involve a social smile, proximity, eye contact, babble or slight movement. The entire sequence must be played within 15 to 20 seconds. After the child has taken his final turn, the adult must *immediately* begin the sequence over and over again. The goal is to play the sequence repetitively for ten minutes. To achieve this, hesitation between the repetitions of the sequence must not last more than two seconds or the child will seize the opportunity to flee.

If you have shortened the routine and are still not having success, look closely at your technique. Scrutinize your turns; alter them in length. Try lengthening the amount of time spent on the reinforcing turn. Look at your level of animation. A tremendous amount of animation and exaggerated movement must accompany your turns. Your change will trigger a change in the child.

> *If the child is not responding, change what you are doing.*

You will know when you finally meet him at his communicative level. He will reward you by "staying" longer. You will finally feel a bridge of communication between the two of you, shaky at first but growing stronger as this foundation is laid.

LET'S IMAGINE

How to speed up the giggle game pace by shortening the game to its three components: predictable sequence, cue and reinforcing turn

EXAMPLE

In the following example, the adult keeps the total joint action routine within four turns. Two turns for the child and two for the adult is the desirable length for a successful giggle game with a child whose staying power is very weak. As his staying power increases, so will the length of his games.

PROBLEM

Shane's staying power is extremely weak. If an adult manages to develop a short routine with him, he appears only to tolerate it one time before quickly making his escape.

SOLUTION

Develop a sequence with Shane that is only 15 to 20 seconds in duration. The entire sequence should be no longer than two adult turns and two child turns. The adult's two turns should be made up of the cue and reinforcer. When the sequence has ended, the adult must not hesitate more than one second before moving right back into the first turn of the sequence, *quickly* repeating the game again and again.

SPIDER

The adult accepts proximity and eye contact as this child's turn since he is primarily working on staying power.

Waiting for a gesture, movement or vocalization may slow down the pace of the game, risking the escape of the child.

Adult: *Whispers with rising inflection.* Spider…spider… spider…spider… *Places hand above child's head and slowly moves it downward toward the child's face, curling and walking fingers as if they are spider legs (cue).*

Child: *Eye contact.*

Adult: Spider's going to get you! (*Reinforcer.*) *Speaks loudly, quickly lunging forward and begins tickling with "spider" fingers.*

Child: *Laughs and pulls "spider" fingers closer to him.*

Quickly **repeat sequence for ten minutes.**

Spider

Spider?...

Spider?...

Spider?...

spider?...

Eye contact will be his turn. His staying power is too weak, so I can't wait for more right now — I might "lose" him.

Adult turn – Cue ("spider" hand above child's head slowly moving towards child's face).
Child turn – Eye contact.

Adult turn – Reinforcer (speaks loudly, lunging forward, begins tickling with "spider" fingers).
Child turn – Pulls "spider" fingers closer and laughs.

Spider's going to get you!

When a child's staying power is extremely weak, the entire sequence should be no longer than two adult and two child turns. The adult's two turns should be made up of the cue and reinforcer.

WHAT? WHEN? WHY?

Answers to common questions

Q. You have talked about following lead and imitation as principal strategies. Why don't I just continue to employ these with a child that has little staying power?

A. Continue to do them. They are wonderful strategies but, in addition, the child needs to develop social reciprocity; the taking of turns in a back and forth manner. Even though it is frustrating, the adult must continually attempt to develop turn taking routines with a child possessing weak staying power. Watching the pace and length of routines will be crucial to the success of building up turn taking with this child.

Q. Why is it important to add sound to my movements?

A. For added interest. Your job is to lengthen the child's staying power. Whether it's seconds or minutes, the silly, exaggerated sounds you make will delay their departure.

Q. I've tried but his staying power is still extremely weak. I feel that he is just not interested in me! What can I do?

A. Be outrageous. Be flamboyant. Be bigger than life. Become the focal point of the room. Become so animated that he can't help but notice, stop a second and watch! Pull his sock over his shoe, his shirt over his head. Toss a pillow at him, run after him, block his path, pick him up and twirl him, pop out at him and blow bubbles in his face, wear a mask and creep up slowly. Keep trying and keep moving. You will find "something" that makes him stop momentarily. When you do, repeat it over and over again as *quickly* as you can, using his fleeting eye contact as his turn.

OBJECTIVES WORKSHEET

Increase staying power by picking up the giggle game pace

CHILD'S NAME_____

CURRENT LEVEL

The adult has been following lead and imitating the child but has not been able to successfully sustain a turn-taking sequence that incorporates a cue and reinforcing turn. The child's staying power is still extremely weak.

Date initiated_____ Date mastered_____

1. Given a short four-turn giggle time routine, the child will remain engaged in the turn-taking interaction for five minutes.

Date initiated_____ Date mastered_____

2. Given a short four-turn giggle time routine, the child will remain engaged in the turn-taking interaction for ten minutes.

3

Expecting More

CHAPTER OVERVIEW

This chapter discusses strategies for enticing the child out of his comfort zone. As the child's communication skills and social reciprocity develop, he may reach a particular stage and level off in his progress. The child may be perfectly happy at this stage, but the adult may feel frustrated, knowing that he is capable of more. The adult may, however, be unsure of how to move the child to a higher level. This chapter offers the reader keys to unlocking the child's hidden potential when more is expected but the child's responses remain the same, day to day and month to month.

Dear Jacob,

I watch you and feel impatient. I can now engage you in giggle games but your ability to communicate on your turn is the same as last month. You have made significant gains but appear to be stuck.

Can you give me more? I truly believe that you can learn to communicate at a higher level. I know that change is hard but it's time to let go of the old. Let me help you move forward. I'll watch you closely. Cue me with your eyes and body language so I will know how far to push. Then we'll move forward, together a team, you and I.

Love,

Miss Sue

*We're all assigned a piece of the garden, a corner of the Universe
that is ours to transform. Our corner of the Universe is our own life
– our relationships, our homes, and our work.*

Marianne Williamson, *A Return to Love*

DELAYING YOUR TURN

KEY POINTS

Think he can do more? Wait expectantly

> If the child is ready to move to a new communicative step, do not attempt it at the beginning of a giggle session. Play the established sequence for five minutes and then begin to wait expectantly for new turns.

> Delaying the reinforcing turn often triggers a new turn from the child.

> The game's predictability must be firmly established before the adult's reinforcing turn is delayed.

There may come a time when you or the child become bored with an established routine. You may wish the child were exhibiting different pragmatic skills on his turn. There are ways to encourage this as an *established* routine is repetitively played. Note, however, that the key word is "established." In order for a routine to become established, it must have been played repetitively over a period of days or weeks. Once it is firmly established and each partner is confident with the predictability of the routine, an attempt to elicit a new pragmatic skill from the child can be made. Delaying your reinforcing turn longer than usual can do this. As you delay, the child is given an expectant look with your eyes and body posture. This delay may elicit the emergence of a new pragmatic language skill on the child's next turn. "Once knowledge of routine structure has been established, delay or discontinuance of an anticipated event often becomes a strong motivator for communication" (Schuler and Prizant 1987). James MacDonald uses the visual image of a staircase to depict levels of communication. He feels that the adult should have one foot on the child's stair step and the other foot on the step above. In this way, the adult can "pull the child up to the next step" (MacDonald 1989). Delaying the adult's turn in a play routine is one way to pull the child up the communication staircase. What is

When the established routine is repetitively played, the child is provided with numerous ending/reinforcing turns.

As the child participates in numerous reinforcing turns, he'll remember why he loves the game. His motivation for continuing the routine with a new turn will be strong when the adult waits and delays the reinforcing turn.

If a new pragmatic skill emerges on his turn today, do not expect it right away tomorrow. The child will need to build up to this new turn, again and again.

the next step? The next step can be any pragmatic communication skill that the child has not yet mastered. The child may:

- display facial/body imitation

- express intent through a variety of means (use of gesture and/or sign to initiate and continue giggle games when they are delayed; establish proximity to staff or giggle game prop; sustain eye contact to aid communication; shift of gaze between adult and movements; vocalize a variety of sounds, word approximations, single words and phrases; effectively bring attention to self)

- string sounds together

- respond to name

- display visual regard by orienting to partner

- display positive affect in response to partner

- engage in a giggle game that focuses on a common theme (e.g., Get You)

- elaborate the turn-taking sequence, adding to the development of the game

- take the lead in how the routine progresses

- join in giggle games with peers

- engage in joint attention; focus on same stimuli that is the focus of the partner

- demonstrate a social smile/laugh

- participate in shared positive affect by demonstrating clear interest and pleasure toward adult

- replace inappropriate interactive turns with socially acceptable forms of communication

- turn head in direction of giggle game sounds

- orient to sudden motion

- tolerate movement in a giggle game

- allow others in personal space

- lead another through imitative turn taking

- develop staying power

- establish reciprocity of turn taking in a back-and-forth manner where child is "reading" the cues of the adult and responding in relation to those cues

- consistently respond in a reciprocal manner

- demonstrate understanding of partner's gestures, facial expressions, eye gaze and intonation cues

- maintain physical contact

- generalize play routines to others

- demonstrate anticipation of game sequences

- repair communicative breakdowns

- combine several intentional behaviors in one game

- imitate sounds/key words

- expand vocabulary

- repeat modeled and prompted vocabulary

- generate novel utterances.

LET'S IMAGINE

Delay your turn to get more from the child

EXAMPLE

The following example depicts how the adult can delay his reinforcing turn in the hope of triggering a different communicative effort from the child.

PROBLEM

In each giggle game that Joshua has played over a six-month period, his turns have consistently been eye contact, remaining in proximity, social smiles, joint attention, laughter, gesture and continuing the movement of the game. Vocalizations have not occurred.

SOLUTION

As an old giggle game is played, the adult must delay the reinforcing turn at the end of the sequence after he sees the child's established turn. Typically, on seeing this turn, the adult would play the reinforcer; however, this time he *waits* for more. He waits for any babble, sound or utterance and, upon hearing it, immediately gives meaning to it by playing the reinforcing turn.

ROUND LIKE A CIRCLE

The first time the adult initially delays the reinforcing turn, the child usually gives his old turn.

When the child gives an old turn, the adult should not respond but wait expectantly instead.

Once the child's new turn emerges, the adult must wait for it again each time the sequence is repeated.

Adult: Round like a circle, like a teddy bear. *Adult slowly moves pointer finger in a circle in child's palm.*

Child: *Social smile.*

Adult: One step! *Adult quickly jumps pointer finger to child's forearm.*

Child: *Joint attention as child and adult look at adult's finger on child's arm.*

Adult: T...w...o s...t...e...p...s... *It is said very slowly and adult jumps the pointer finger up the child's arm to the crease of the elbow joint (cue).*

Child: *Joint attention, looking at adult's finger in anticipation.*

Adult: (*Delay*) *Waits expectantly by leaning and positioning hand in a tickling position.*

Child: Tih. *Previous turn was a social smile.*

Adult: *Loudly* Tickle under there! *Adult moves pointer finger up the child's arm and tickles child's armpit (reinforcer).*

Repeat sequence for ten minutes.

Round Like a Circle

Round like a circle,
Like a teddy bear,
One step,
Twoooo stehhhhhps...

The adult has chosen to slow down the phrasing to cue the child that the reinforcing turn is coming.

He's trying to say tickle!

Tih!

The best time to wait expectantly is after the cue. That's when the child may "give" more on his turn.

Tickle under there!

WHAT? WHEN? WHY?

Answers to common questions

Q. How do I get the child to make a sound or vocalization? I would like to move him to a higher level. He is so silent.

A. Listen closely throughout the joint action routine for any sound that happens by chance. Repeat it back to the child and immediately assign meaning to it by quickly performing the reinforcing turn. Then, in the next repetition, when you come to that same point in the routine, delay your turn and wait expectantly. Once again, verbally prompt that sound to the child several times and wait. You may elicit that sound again. However, take any sound. It doesn't have to be the same one.

Q. How will I know if I am expecting a turn that is too high for the child at this time?

A. The child will let you know. He will turn away or leave.

Q. How will I know if it is the right time to expect more from the child?

A. The right time is when the game is firmly established, each player knows the sequence, and the child loves the routine and desperately wants the interaction to continue.

Q. If I try to pull him up to another pragmatic skill and he doesn't change his turn, will I lose the momentum of the game?

A. No, not if you wait 10 to 15 seconds for a new response and, when you don't receive it, return to the original sequence. Try again after a few more repetitions of the original routine.

Q. I have heard the child repeat words after me throughout other parts of the day when he desires food or toys. However, I have tried to no avail to get him to say "down" in our "Ring Around the Rosy" game. He has not yet used words on his turn in a joint action routine.

A. You cannot push this. You can verbally prompt the desired word, look expectantly, and delay the reinforcing turn, but you must eventually take the turn that he gives you or you will lose him. Softly, verbally prompt "down" several times. Position your mouth in the beginning sound of the word and look expectantly at the child. Persevere, eventually a new turn will come and it will take you by surprise!

Q. Why must I delay the reinforcing turn to elicit a new pragmatic skill in the routine? Can't I delay any one of my turns?

A. The reinforcing turn is the most powerful turn of the sequence. Since it comes last, the child will have a difficult time holding back his excitement and anticipation. This will entice him to work harder on his turn so that you will finish the routine.

OBJECTIVES WORKSHEET

Expect more and receive more by delaying the reinforcing turn

CHILD'S NAME _____

CURRENT LEVEL

This child enjoys giggle time but tends to have the same communicative turns for each giggle game.

Date initiated_____ Date mastered_____

1. Given an established giggle game that is stopped before the reinforcing turn and an adult who moves their face and body closer to the child in expectation, the child will continue the game through a new vocalization, touch, or movement.

Date initiated_____ Date mastered_____

2. Given an established giggle game and a delay in the adult's reinforcing turn, the child will exhibit a new pragmatic language skill on one of his turns.

Date initiated_____ Date mastered_____

3. Given an established giggle game that is stopped before the reinforcing turn and an adult who softly verbally prompts the next word, the child will continue the game by positioning his lips in the beginning sound of the next word, stating a word approximation or vocalizing a new sound.

Every moment we have the opportunity to "change the future by reprogramming the present."

Marianne Williamson, *A Return to Love*

REPEATING THE CUE

KEY POINTS

Still not changing? Repeat, repeat, repeat then wait

> *Expecting more from the child demands perseverance and a great deal of patience.*

> *If a new turn does not develop the first time it's attempted, take what the child gives and try again.*

> *If the child gives an approximation of a higher turn, quickly play the reinforcing turn of the routine. Be confident that a higher skill is slowly emerging. Continue to take the approximation for a while.*

Sometimes it takes more than delaying the reinforcing turn to elicit a higher turn from the child. The child needs to sense that you are expecting something different on his turn. He also needs a sense of growing anticipation and increased excitement from you, more than in the original routine! This is best accomplished by repeating the cue three times and waiting with heightened expectancy between each repetition for the child's new turn.

Heightened expectancy means that there must be a high level of expectation in your voice, indicated by a rise in your inflection. It also means that you must hold an exaggerated body posture and facial expression. Attempt to actually "freeze" your expression and posture at the end of each cue, leaving your mouth, eyes, and limbs in an exaggerated open position. Also, elongate the sound of the cue more than usual, taking several breaths as you continue. Thus, you will make it more and more noticeable to the child that you are near the ending of the routine but are waiting for his turn so you may continue. With hope, a new turn!

LET'S IMAGINE

Repeat the cue to receive more from the child

EXAMPLE

The following example demonstrates that the child will often manufacture a new turn in an established game if the cue is repeated with increased animation.

PROBLEM

Joseph appears to be stuck. His established games have become boring and it's time to move him out of his comfort level.

SOLUTION

The cue will be repeated by the adult at least three times in anticipation of a new response from the child.

HIPPITY HOPPITY HOO

Adult: *Child is sitting on adult's lap, face to face, holding hands. Child is bounced on knees to rhythm of words:* Hippity Hoppity Hoo.

Child: *Eye contact. Both move together in circular motion while still holding hands.*

Adult: I'm going to,

Child: *Social smile.*

Adult: *Continues holding hands while raising child's arms up slowly over his head. G...e...t... With rising inflection (first cue).*

Child: *Eye contact. This is the child's old turn. The adult expects more and will now begin repeating the cue.*

Each time the cue is repeated, increase the exaggeration and animation.

Adult: *Brings child's arms back down, moves head closer, sticks neck out and opens eyes wide with anticipation. Lifts child's arms up slowly over his head once again. "G...e...t" With rising inflection and increased volume (second cue).*

Child: *Eye contact.*

> Pair each repetition of the cue with a sudden jerky movement to keep the child's attention.

Adult: *Brings child's arms back down, moves head in close again, eyes wide, and lifts arms up again but this time with jerky movements to gain increased attention.* "G......e......t" *Accompanies the cue with rising inflection and increased volume, maintaining the word throughout several breaths* (third cue).

Child: Mmm. *New turn.*

Adult: you! *Tickles child under arms* (reinforcer).

Child: *Laughs.*

Sequence is repeated for ten minutes.

Hippity Hoppity Hoo

Is it time to move the child out of his comfort level? Repeat the cue with increasingly more exaggeration and wait expectantly to get movement up the communication ladder.

WHAT? WHEN? WHY?

Answers to common questions

Q. I noticed that you added jerky movements the third time you repeated the cue in "Hippity Hoppity Hoo." Do you find that adding additional movement is helpful?

A. Most of the time I will add a quick movement as I repeat the cue because I sense the child's attention slipping away. Sometimes, as the routine is delayed by the cue's repetition, the child may sense that something is different and may turn away, avert eye gaze and appear as though they want to leave. The additional movement not only startles them but also brings their attention back to you and the giggle time routine.

Q. I just don't see how I can exaggerate my face, tone, or body posture any more than I already am doing! Do I have to continually increase my exaggeration each time I repeat the cue?

A. You may not have to repeat the cue three times to get a higher turn from the child. You may repeat it once and get a desired response from the child. Further exaggeration is suggested in order to keep the child from losing interest as you wait for a higher turn. It is such hard work for the child to move to a higher level of communication. Also, he is wondering why you are not moving on to the reinforcing turn and completing the sequence. He may give up or feel that the routine is over if you don't find a way to be more animated. You must act quickly with greater intensity each time. Develop your skills. You have the playfulness inside you. Reach within and stretch, just as you are asking the child to do.

OBJECTIVES WORKSHEET

Exhibits a new communicative turn when adult repeats the cue

CHILD'S NAME_____

CURRENT LEVEL

This child enjoys many giggle games but tends to have the same communicative turns for each one.

Date initiated_____ Date mastered_____

1. Given an established giggle time routine and the cue repeated three times by the adult, the child will exhibit a new communicative turn.

Date initiated_____ Date mastered_____

2. Given an established giggle time routine and the cue repeated once by the adult, the child will exhibit a new communicative turn.

...if a sadness rises up before you larger than any you have ever seen; if a restiveness, like light and cloud-shadows, passes over your hands and over all you do. You must think that something is happening to you, that life has not forgotten you, that it holds you in its hand; it will not let you fall.

Rainer Maria Rilke, *Letters to a Young Poet*

DROPPING A WORD

KEY POINTS

Is his turn still the same? Omit your ending word

> As you omit the ending word of a phrase, drop all movement and wait expectantly.

> You may drop the ending word of a phrase on one or several of your turns.

> Give immediate feedback to the child by repeating what he said before you take your next turn.

> Take an emergence of a higher skill as a new turn, and then refine it at a later date.

If the child has not yet developed a new pragmatic skill on one of his turns, you may want to try the following technique. Choose a favored routine that is highly predictable to the child. As you play your turn, drop the ending word of one of your phrases and wait expectantly. If the child does not respond within eight to ten seconds, repeat the phrase once again with the ending word omitted. As you drop the word, also stop any movement. This will signal the child that something is changing.

As he sees you waiting expectantly, he may feel the urge to help you along. He may say the omitted word, a word approximation, beginning sound, and a vocalization, or he may make a silent mouth movement. Take what he gives you, repeat it back and then immediately reinforce his new effort by continuing the routine.

It is important to accept the emergence of a higher skill as a new turn. It can be shaped and refined at a later date when it has been repetitively played as a new turn in the routine. Remember that moving up the communication ladder is difficult and we must be careful to applaud the emergence of a higher communication skill.

LET'S IMAGINE

How to drop a word and receive a new communicative turn

EXAMPLE

The following example demonstrates how the ending word of a familiar phrase can be dropped to induce a new sound or gesture.

PROBLEM

Justin enjoys many giggle games with adults and has begun to vocalize intermittently throughout the day to aid his requests. However, his turns in joint action routines have remained nonvocal.

SOLUTION

Play his favorite giggle game and drop the ending word of the phrase that is paired with the cue. He will be more apt to try to fill in the missing word with a new turn. He will try to hurry along the game to get to his favorite part, the reinforcing turn.

ONE POTATO

Adult: *Child lies on his back on a mat. The adult leans over child, holding child's hands throughout the routine. Adult places child's right hand on the mat next to his head.* One potato.

Child: *Eye contact.*

Adult: *Child's left hand is placed on the left side of his body.* Two potato. *Child's right hand crosses body to left waist.* Three potato. *Child's left hand crosses body to right waist.* Four potato.

Child: *Eye contact.*

Adult: Five potato. *Adult moves child's left hand above his left shoulder.* Six potato. *Adult moves his right hand above his right shoulder.*

Child: *Social smile.*

Adult: *Moves both of child's hands in a shaky movement, slowly raising them above his head.* S...e...v...e...n

> *Once the approximation of a new turn is established for a period of time, the adult can begin to shape and refine it.*

p...o...t...a...t...o...o...o...o [*drop last word of cued phrase*] *said with rising inflection, holding the ending sound.*

Child: Moh. *Child says a word approximation of "more," which is a new turn.*

Adult: More! *Nuzzles child on chest with forehead/hair (reinforcer).*

Child: *Laughs.*

Sequence is repeated for ten minutes.

One Potato

...Five potato,
Six potato,

se– ven

poh–tay–**tooooh...**

(wait)

I'll accept the approximation of the word "more" as his turn. Now I'll quickly take my turn in the routine and provide the reinforcer that he loves.

Moh

Drop the ending word in a favorite giggle game
phrase to pull the child up the communication ladder.

WHAT? WHEN? WHY?

Answers to common questions

Q. When the adult is expecting more from the child and drops one word from a phrase, does he have to drop the ending word?

A. As you recite the beginning and middle of a familiar phrase, you provide the child with a verbal cue that the end of the phrase is coming. Since the joint action routine has been repetitively played on numerous occasions, the child anticipates the complete phrase. When the adult delays the ending word it encourages the child to fill in the blank, furthering the social connection.

Q. How do I decide if a phrase of a giggle game can be used in this way?

A. There are several things to consider when choosing a phrase to drop words from. The game, from which the phrase is taken, must be a favorite of the child's. The reinforcer must be highly motivating. Also, a phrase should be chosen that has an accompanying action. The movement will also cue him and he will be even more inclined to know what word comes next when you suddenly delay a word. With these things in mind, moving him toward a higher level is not only possible but also highly probable.

Q. How many times can I drop an ending word during a giggle game?

A. Try one phrase and if the child fills in the missing word then drop the ending word of another phrase. However, the child may enjoy this adaptation of an old routine but may not have the word retrieval necessary to retrieve the ending word of several phases. You can verbally prompt, as needed, by whispering the desired word and then waiting expectantly. Once again, take any approximation in the beginning. You may wonder if you are pushing too hard. The key is to follow the child's cues. Watch, wait, and listen. The child will provide the information you need. He will let you know if you are too high by his body posture, averted eye gaze, restlessness, and lack of staying power. You will also begin to feel an air of tension and anxiety if you are asking too much. If you are, it's time for you to return to the full phrase in that portion of the rhyme. Expect a little more but continue to follow his lead and let him guide you.

OBJECTIVES WORKSHEET

Exhibit a new communicative turn when adult drops a word of a phrase

CHILD'S NAME_____

CURRENT LEVEL
This child enjoys many giggle games but tends to have the same communicative turns for each one.

Date initiated_____ Date mastered_____

1. Given an established giggle game and the adult dropping one word from a phrase, the child will signal the adult to continue by displaying a new gesture or movement.

Date initiated_____ Date mastered_____

2. Given an established giggle game and the adult dropping one word from a phrase, the child will signal the adult to continue by silently moving his mouth in the shape of a sound.

Date initiated_____ Date mastered_____

3. Given an established giggle game and the adult dropping one word from a phrase, the child will signal the adult to continue by babbling any sound.

Date initiated_____ Date mastered_____

4. Given an established giggle game and the adult dropping one word from a phrase, the child will signal the adult to continue by stating the missing word or word approximation of it.

4

Encouraging Initiation

CHAPTER OVERVIEW

This chapter will discuss ways to encourage the child's initiation of their favorite giggle games in socially acceptable ways. Props, photos, seizing the moment and physical prompting will be utilized to assist this goal.

Dear Jacob,

For weeks, I have been approaching you and initiating our giggle games. We have truly bonded in these sessions, enjoying the connection we have found. However, when we are not engaged, I search for you and find you isolated once again. You seem to immediately revert back to studying the angles and lines of the objects in the room, oblivious to those around you. Other times, you suddenly race through the school hallway, and when I call "Jacob Stop! Come!" you laugh and run in the opposite direction.

You are attempting to engage me in a chasing game but you are initiating interaction in an inappropriate way. It reminds me of others who have hit or pulled hair in an attempt to interact. You must learn, as they have, to successfully initiate by requesting the giggle games you love.

I can give meaning to your behaviors and help you develop your communication attempts in a way that not only I, but also others, will understand and respond favorably to. Continue to stand near a prop that we have used in our games, pat it, look at it, and walk by it. I will watch you closely and this time...I'll be ready.

Love,

Miss Sue

Have you ever really had a teacher? One who saw you as a raw but precious thing, a jewel that, with wisdom, could be polished to a proud shine? If you are lucky enough to find your way to such teachers, you will always find your way back.

Mitch Albom, *Tuesdays with Morrie*

SEIZING THE MOMENT

KEY POINTS

He's initiating interaction by hitting me and smiling. How do I get him to initiate interaction in socially acceptable ways?

> *Watch the child closely.*

> *Behaviors occur throughout the day that can be shaped and reinforced to aid the child's initiation of turn taking routines.*

> *Each time a positive emerging behavior is seen, it must be acted upon immediately.*

> *The child may not be at the illocutionary level of bringing an adult a prop or pulling an adult to one.*

The key to encouraging initiation of a giggle game is having an observant eye and then seizing the moment. The adult must consistently "catch" the child exhibiting a behavior that might be interpreted as a signal to begin a game. Standing near an object, momentarily sitting on it, patting it, picking it up, making a gesture, movement or sound, are but a few examples of behaviors that can be seized.

When looking for behaviors to seize, it is helpful to understand the first two levels of communicative intent. It is in the "First Level, Proactive Perlocutionary or Preintentional," that the adult will find a multitude of incidental behaviors, actions, gestures and sounds in which to assign the communicative meaning of initiation. At this level, the child is "not yet directing vocal or gestural signals to others nor is he anticipating specific social outcomes contingent upon his behavior." His behaviors are random.

As the adult consistently assigns meaning to these incidental behaviors, the child will move into the "Primitive Illocutionary or Early Intentional Phase of Level One." He may want an interaction to begin but may not consistently display the verbal/nonverbal communication strategies that are necessary for accomplishing that goal. "He may begin to direct signals expecting specific outcomes" (Prizant 1984), but may become frustrated if his attempts break down and he lacks the persistence to repair them. Either way, in Level One, the child is not successfully initiating a social interaction through his favored giggle games. He must be taught how to effectively do so.

> *Communicative intent or meaning is assigned to the behavior each time it is reinforced by your response.*

If the adult sees an action or hears a sound, and reinforces the behavior each time by seizing the moment, meaning will be assigned. Incidental behaviors will soon become communicative behaviors with intent. At this point, the child has moved into "Level Two, Conventional Illocutionary or Intentional," communication. He will

> have a clear concept of non-verbal communication. He will use conventional gestural and vocal means to affect others" behavior and achieve specific outcomes. His signals will be understood by a wider range of people and he will demonstrate great persistence if his communication goals are not met. (Prizant 1984)

Each time the adult assigns meaning, it shows the child that because he did (*behavior, action, gesture or vocalization*), the adult came over and did (*a turn-taking giggle game sequence*). That is why it is so important to seize this moment throughout the day, reinforcing the behavior *each time* it's seen. The adult must drop what he is doing, run to the child, repeat the title of the game and play the sequence. The adult should try to engage the child in at least three repetitions of the sequence before returning to a previous task.

How will the adult know if it's time to shape behaviors as an initiation of giggle time routines? She will know if she can answer "yes" to the following questions. Does the child *continue* routines when an adult intermittently stops them? Does he *enjoy* an assortment of giggle games with several adults? Does the adult *always* initiate the games? Has the child ever tried to *engage* an adult in an interaction, either through appropriate or inappropriate means? If so, he is ready to move up the communication ladder. He has developed social reciprocity, but he must now learn how to effectively and appropriately initiate his favorite games with the adults in his life. Each communicative attempt is like a fragile sprout trying desperately to emerge into the light. Neglect or ignore it and it will die. Feed it with attention and it will thrive. As the weak initiating behavior is reinforced and becomes stronger, it will occur more and more often. It will move from a perlocutionary behavior to an acquired intentional illocutionary communicative act.

LET'S IMAGINE

How to assign communicative meaning to random movements and vocalizations

EXAMPLE 1

In example 1 the teacher is engaged with a child in an alphabet task at a table. She looks up and sees another child crawl into the play tunnel. She hands the alphabet task to another adult and runs to the tunnel. The tunnel is a prop used in an ABC giggle game between this adult and child. This example is an illustration of how the adult must momentarily drop an activity to reinforce a child's random behavior, shaping it into an initiation communicative skill.

PROBLEM

Jen wanders around the periphery of the room, rarely staying in one area for any length of time. She lacks action in object play during unstructured time. She has developed giggle games with adults and continues them when they are momentarily stopped, but has never effectively initiated one during giggle time or free time.

SOLUTION

When Jen is seen near a prop that is used in a giggle game, the adult needs to stop what she is doing, run over and begin that particular game. This will increase the child's proximity to this particular game prop in the future. As this is repetitively done, she will begin to anticipate the adult coming over when she is near the prop and will begin to use eye gaze toward the adult. When this happens, it indicates that the child is moving up the communication ladder and this communication strategy should be reinforced. Watching for the child to establish proximity to the prop, but waiting for the emerging eye gaze from the child before running over, will give meaning to her eye gaze as an initiating behavior and its frequency will increase. As proximity to the game prop and eye gaze are reinforced, the child will develop several tools for effectively initiating a giggle game.

 ABC

Repeat the title of the game with a questioning inflection as you approach the child near a game prop.	Child: *Sitting quietly in tunnel.*
	Adult: ABC? *Peeks into tunnel.*
	Child: *Looks with anticipation at tunnel opening.*
	Adult: A…B…C…D…E…F… *Each letter is recited softly as she rocks the tunnel back and forth. When she gets to the letter "f" she suddenly stops talking (cue).*
Momentarily stop what you are doing and apply meaning to a behavior or movement.	Child: G.
	Adult: *Loudly exclaims* G! *Quickly lunges in toward child and tickles (reinforcer).*
Engage the child for three repetitions of the giggle game before returning to your original task.	Child: *Laughs, eye contact.*
	Adult: *Laughs, eye contact.*
	Routine is repeated three times before adult returns to original task.

LET'S IMAGINE

How to assign communicative meaning to random movements and vocalizations

EXAMPLE 2

In example 2, the adult is engaged in a "Ring Around the Rosy" giggle game with a child. She looks up and sees Melanie twirling in a circle. "Ring Around the Rosy" is a joint action routine that is also played with Melanie who, however,

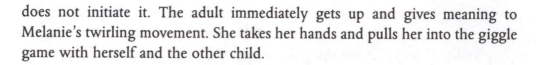

does not initiate it. The adult immediately gets up and gives meaning to Melanie's twirling movement. She takes her hands and pulls her into the giggle game with herself and the other child.

PROBLEM

Melanie happily engages in giggle games with adults but does not initiate them. She is often observed twirling or running back and forth throughout the room.

SOLUTION

Create giggle games with Melanie that involve circular movements and running. Watch for these random movements during free time and if they slightly mimic a movement in an established giggle game, drop what you are doing, run over and play the established game three times.

 ROSY

> Adult: Rosy? Play Rosy?
>
> Child: *Eye contact. Holds adult's hands and moves in circle with her and the other child.*
>
> **Routine is repeated three times before adult returns to original task.**

LET'S IMAGINE

How to assign communicative meaning to random movements and vocalizations

EXAMPLE 3

In example 3, the adult is setting up an art activity. She glances across the room and sees a child, Sebastian, in an area of the room where they always play the "Blast Off!" game. He exhibits a quick glance in her direction. She immediately drops what she is doing, runs over to the child and assumes the game's body position, seizing the moment.

PROBLEM

Sebastian does not yet effectively initiate his favorite giggle games. At times, he has slapped an adult or pulled their hair to initiate an interaction. Eye contact is fleeting.

SOLUTION

The adult watches for any behavior that could be "read" and interpreted as a positive step toward initiation. When the adult observes the child's location and catches his eye contact, she drops what she is doing and asks him if he wants to play. She reinforces the eye contact from across the room as a step toward initiating a playful interaction in a positive way.

 ONE... TWO... THREE... BLAST OFF!

> Adult: One...Two...Three?
>
> Child: *Eye contact, on back looking up, remains in proximity.*
>
> Adult: *Begins a joint action routine that has been played numerous times with this child in this body position. The adult lies on her back and positions the child on the fronts of her legs. She softly chants* One...Two... Three... *as a cue. After receiving a turn from the child, she raises him high into the air on her legs while shouting* Blast Off! *She continues three repetitions before resuming her previous task.*

LET'S IMAGINE

How to assign communicative meaning to random movements and vocalizations

EXAMPLE 4

In this example, the teacher and students are on community-based instruction, in a store setting. One child makes a random airplane sound. No eye contact with the adult is noted.

PROBLEM

Johnny is very difficult to engage in a joint action routine. His staying power is two to three seconds and he has very few joint action routines established. His giggle time consists primarily of gross motor imitation throughout the room.

SOLUTION

The adult attempts to apply meaning to one of his random sounds and develop a turn-taking routine. Johnny and the adult continue the newly established routine for at least ten minutes as they move through the community setting. When they return to the classroom, the adult makes the airplane sound and movement of her finger to demonstrate that the game can be generalized across various settings. By seizing the moment and giving the sound consistent attention, initiation is apt to occur on subsequent days. Thus, each time the adult hears that particular sound, the moment must be seized and the routine begun.

AIRPLANE

Child: *Random airplane sound.*

Adult: *Imitates the airplane sound.*

Child: *Eye contact and interest.*

Adult: *Imitates the airplane sound again and adds the motion of index finger slowly coming in for a "landing" under the child's chin (cue).*

Child: *Social smile, eye contact.*

Adult: *Imitates the airplane sound again, continues the index finger landing and adds a tickle under the chin (reinforcer).*

Child: *Laughs.*

Adult: *Laughs. Looks with expectation toward child. Visually prompts by placing finger in air and waiting.*

Child: *Makes airplane sound.*

Adult: *Imitates airplane sound, finger comes in for a "landing" and tickles.*

Child: *Laughs.*

Adult: *Laughs.*

LET'S IMAGINE

How to assign communicative meaning to random movements and vocalizations

EXAMPLE 5

In this example, the adult and child are taking a walk around the block. The child begins to hiccup. The adult builds a giggle game out of the child's hiccups.

PROBLEM

Damien has very little staying power. He does not remain in a giggle game for an extended amount of time. He never initiates an interaction.

SOLUTION

This is a wonderful game for a child with little staying power. The child does not have control over his hiccups and has no choice but to continue the game! The first turn of the routine is his hiccup. Every time he hiccups over the next few days or weeks, he will be initiating this game. The adult can also initiate the game by pretending to hiccup.

 HICCUP!

Child: *Randomly makes a hiccup sound.*

Adult: What was that, was it you?

Child: *Eye contact.*

Adult: *Stops walking (cue).*

Child: *Eye contact.*

Adult: *Lunges down and tosses child gently back and forth (reinforcer).*

Child: *Laughs.*

Adult: *Resumes walking. Waits for next hiccup and continues the game for as long as the hiccups last.*

Blast Off!

The adult sees the child establish eye contact and move to the area of the room where they play "One…Two…Three…Blast-Off!" She seizes the moment, assigning meaning to the behaviors by dropping what she was doing and engaging the child in the game.

WHAT? WHEN? WHY?

Answers to common questions

Q. What if the child continually engages in an emerging initiating behavior and I have to keep dropping my task to reinforce it time and time again? I won't get other tasks done.

A. No other task is as important as shaping and reinforcing an emerging communication skill. It needs to be a priority and something that you are constantly on the lookout for as you gaze around the room, especially when you are in the midst of other tasks. You will be happy that you did when you see that it leads to an initiation of a routine by the child at a later date.

Q. Why would I drop what I am doing to reinforce a child patting a prop? It doesn't look like initiation to me.

A. Remember that you must accept the communication level of the child and build upon it. If establishing proximity to the prop by patting it is the closest he has come to initiating a routine, then you must place one foot on his step of the communication ladder and pull him up to the next rung. When you run over to him, say, "want [*name of game*]?" and begin the routine.

Q. How do I reinforce an emerging initiating behavior if it occurs for just a few seconds and then the child quickly moves to another part of the room?

A. Move quickly! Jump over tables if you have to. As you run, say "[*child's name, title of game*]?" Repeat this question over and over as you move across the room toward the child. Try to move the child back to the prop or move the prop to the child. Repeat the child's name and title of game. Begin the joint action routine as soon as you can, repeating the game three times. You must be careful not to reinforce another behavior that the child will pair with your response.

Q. When you observe an emerging initiating behavior and "run over" to reinforce it, why does the sequence need to be replayed at least three times before returning to your previous task?

A. You want the child to understand that you came to play that particular routine because of the behavior he exhibited. Since a routine sequence is typically very short, repeating it at least three times gives the child sustained attention and reinforces the emerging behavior. If it was played for just a few seconds, the child might feel like you just "happened by," not understanding how he influenced your behavior. This sustained interaction increases the likelihood that he will connect his behavior to yours. "When I do this, she does that." It is imperative that, once you return to your original task, you watch closely for the same behavior so it can be reinforced again.

Q. Do you have to return to your original task or can you just continue to play the routine for ten minutes?

A. Return to the original task so that you give the child an opportunity to exhibit and practice the emerging initiating behavior. Thus, it will be reinforced with greater frequency. The higher the frequency of reinforcement, the more likely the behavior will become embedded in the child's communication repertoire.

Q. Why is it important to say the title of the game as I begin the game sequence?

A. Perhaps the child will develop language and use it in combination with nonverbal strategies to initiate an interaction. You are offering a model to the child. Through your verbal prompt, the child may eventually repeat what you have said, thus increasing his communication tools and effectiveness.

OBJECTIVES WORKSHEET

Seize the moment in order to encourage the child's initiation of giggle games

CHILD'S NAME_____

CURRENT LEVEL

This child enjoys a variety of giggle games and displays adequate staying power. He does not yet initiate games with adults through establishing proximity, making a game movement, gesture and/or vocalization.

Date initiated_____ Date mastered_____

1. Given an adult and another child playing a highly desired giggle game, the child will establish proximity to the pair. (The adult assigns meaning to the child coming near the pair by pulling him into the existing game.)

Date initiated_____ Date mastered_____

2. Given a movement that is indicative of an established giggle game and the adult joining him, the child will engage in the routine.

Date initiated_____ Date mastered_____

3. The child will initiate a giggle game by making a game sound in an adult's presence.

Date initiated_____ Date mastered_____

4. Child will increase the number of giggle games he initiates with an adult to three.

Date initiated_____ Date mastered_____

5. Given the child's desire to initiate a favored giggle game, he will refrain from inappropriate behaviors and make his request known through appropriate means of touch, gesture, vocalization, movement and/or proximity.

*Be patient with all that is unresolved in your heart and try to love
the questions themselves like locked rooms and like books that are
written in a very foreign tongue. Do not now seek the answers…
Live the questions now. Perhaps you will then gradually, without
noticing it, live along some distant day into the answer.*

Rainer Maria Rilke, *Letters to a Young Poet*

USING PROPS

KEY POINTS

I don't see movements or hear vocalizations that I can assign meaning to. How will I shape initiation?

> The prop provides a visual reminder of the routine.

If the adult doesn't see movements or hear vocalizations that she can assign meaning to and the child is not yet initiating giggle games, then incorporating game props into new routines will aid this dilemma. The use of game props will create more opportunities for the adult to shape initiation. Without a prop, the adult must wait for random movements and vocalizations and then assign meaning to them in order to shape initiating behaviors. However, passive children may not exhibit many vocalizations and movements, thus limiting opportunities for interpretation. With props, the child merely has to establish proximity to one, regardless of intent. The adult then seizes the moment and gives meaning to that behavior by beginning the game that uses that particular object.

> Apply meaning to a behavior exhibited near a prop by quickly reinforcing it with a giggle game.

> Reinforce the behavior near the prop each time it is seen.

> Reinforce it quickly before the child engages in a different behavior.

A prop can be used to encourage the child's initiation of a game since it provides the child with a visual cue. The child may remember the game each time the prop is in view. He may stand next to the prop. He may also walk near it, pause, and then keep moving. He may pick it up, pat it briefly, stand on it or even make the movement of the game for a few seconds. If he sees it used in play with another child, he may establish

> *Play giggle games that incorporate object props.*

> *Each time the giggle game is played, utilize the same prop.*

proximity, even as far as six feet away. Once an initiating objective has been set, it is imperative that all new routines are built around props. Seesaws, rocking horses, merry-go-rounds, parachutes, bolsters, rocking chairs, rolling chairs, scooter boards, feather dusters, forts, boxes, slides, and pillows are examples of props that routines can be built around. Continue playing established routines that involve props as well.

LET'S IMAGINE

Use props in the room to encourage initiation of giggle games by the child

EXAMPLE

The following example demonstrates how to momentarily drop an activity to reinforce a child's behavior by giving meaning to it. It demonstrates one way of shaping a behavior into a communicative request for initiating a giggle game. In this example, the child establishes proximity to a game prop.

PROBLEM

Brandon is very passive. He will now continue a giggle game when the adult plays it repetitively three to four times and suddenly stops. He does not, however, begin a favored game on his own. Even during free time he wanders throughout the room until an adult seeks him out and initiates a play routine.

SOLUTION

Intermittently, throughout the day, engage him in a favored giggle game that involves a prop. Leave the game prop in the center of the room, in full view, when not in use. Whenever he goes near it, pats it, moves it, or displays interest in any way, act upon that action by dropping what you are doing and playing the game. Especially watch for eye gaze in your direction as he establishes proximity.

 KING OF THE CASTLE

Child: *Walks over to bolster and stands next to it.*

Adult: *Engaged in art activity. Observes child. Hands art activity to another staff member and runs over to bolster.* [Child's name] want King of the Castle?

Repeats this question several times as the bolster is set on end and moves the child into position for the routine.

Adult: *Places child on top of bolster in a sitting position. Holds upper torso of child. Sways child and bolster from side to side.* I'm the king of the castle. I'm the king of the castle.

Child: *Social smile.*

Adult: I'm...the...king...of...THE... (*cue*)

Child: castle

Adult: castle! *Tips bolster slightly so child falls into a pool of balls (reinforcer).*

Child: *Social smile.*

Adult: Castle, castle, castle! *Tickles child each time the word "castle" is repeated.*

Child: *Laughs.*

Adult: *Laughs.*

Repeats sequence three times before returning to art activity. Continues to closely observe child and wait for emerging behavior to occur again.

> Keep object props used in giggle games within easy reach of the child throughout the day to encourage initiation, then watch and wait.

> When a behavior that can be shaped as initiation is observed, drop your activity, run to the child, repeat the title of the game in a questioning tone and play the game three times.

WHAT? WHEN? WHY?

Answers to common questions

Q. How will I know if it is time to shape the initiating behavior of a child? How will I know if he is ready?

A. Do not expect a child who does not "continue" a joint action routine when it is intermittently stopped by an adult to initiate a routine completely out of context. The following pragmatic skills are strong indicators that shaping initiating behavior will be successful and will lead to independent initiation by the child: the child has adequate staying power, the child continues a routine when it is intermittently stopped for a few seconds and several highly desirable joint action routines involving props have been developed with the child.

Q. What are some examples of emerging initiating behaviors that I should watch for?

A. The child may stand next to or within three feet of a prop that is used in one of his joint action routines. He may walk by a prop and briefly hesitate before walking on. He may carry a prop around the room for a few minutes. He may pat it or get on it for a few seconds. He may even go near it and quickly glance in your direction.

Q. What are some examples of props that can be used in giggle time routines?

A. A merry-go-round, hula hoop, spinning board or rolling chair might be used as a prop in a "Ring Around the Rosy" routine. A rocking horse or rowboat could be used in a "Row, Row, Row the Boat" routine. You might place a child on a bolster or large ball and engage in a "Humpty Dumpty" routine. A clubhouse, scarf, parachute, blanket, sheet, barrel, pillow or tunnel could be used in a "Peek-a-Boo" or "All Around the Cobbler's Bench" routine.

Q. Can more than one child use the same prop?

A. Yes, this encourages group play. As other children see the prop in use, they may establish proximity and you can "pull" them into the routine as well.

Q. What do I do if a child establishes proximity to a prop and me when I am engaged in a joint action routine with another child?

A. Bring the newly arrived child into the routine by placing your arm tightly around him, placing him on your lap, or positioning him on the prop with the other child. Then *quickly* continue the routine without missing a word or beat of the rhyme. If you hesitate, you may lose them both.

OBJECTIVES WORKSHEET

Use game props to encourage initiation

CHILD'S NAME_____

CURRENT LEVEL

This child enjoys many joint action routines with adults, many of which involve an object prop. He waits for the adult to initiate established giggle games with him. He may initiate interaction through negative means.

Date initiated_____ Date mastered_____

1. Given giggle game props in his visual field, the child will initiate a giggle game through the use of a game prop and decrease negative means of interaction.

Date initiated_____ Date mastered_____

2. Given game props visible in the room, the child will establish proximity to a prop by standing next to it, touching it or posing on it. (Once child establishes proximity, adult gives meaning to this behavior, thus increasing the probability of initiation at another time.)

Date initiated_____ Date mastered_____

3. Given game props visible in the room, the child will initiate an established routine by bringing a game prop to an adult or by pulling an adult to a prop.

Date initiated_____ Date mastered_____

4. Given a giggle time routine involving a prop, once it is stopped and the adult walks three feet away the child will continue the interaction by vocalizing, pulling the adult back to the prop or making the movement of the game. (This is a training phase possibly leading the child toward initiating this routine through one of these three means at a later time.)

You are not here merely to make a living. You are here to enable the world to live more amply, with greater vision, and with a finer spirit of hope and achievement. You are here to enrich the world.

Woodrow Wilson

PHYSICAL PROMPTS

KEY POINTS

Is he ever going to initiate? He just stands there!

Physical prompting involves very light hand-over-hand guidance for a specific purpose. The child does 99 percent of the movement himself.

Physical prompting can involve two adults and the child or one adult and the child.

Physical prompting during giggle time involves hand-over-hand manipulation of a child's hand within an adult's hand for a specific purpose. It helps the child move his body, giving him a "jump start" in motor planning. When done with a minimal amount of pressure, it allows the child to "feel" the movement and gain an understanding kinesthetically of what is expected. Once a game with a prop has been established, there are several ways to physically prompt a child toward initiating or requesting this giggle game from an adult. The child can be physically prompted, using two adults, or physically prompted by one adult, you.

When two adults are involved, the first adult *silently* moves behind the child, gently guiding him toward the second adult. On reaching him, the first adult places the child's hand within the hand of the second adult and helps the child gently pull. With the aid of the first adult, the child "leads" the second adult over to a favored game prop. The second adult feigns surprise, stating the name of the routine in a question form several times: "[*Name of game, child's name*]?" This procedure can be used with varying distances of one foot, three feet, six feet, or across the room. Each time the first adult aids the child in requesting a giggle game from a second adult, his "aid" should gradually lessen.

Eventually only a nudge in the second adult's direction or moving the child's arm toward the second adult will produce the desired response.

When you are the only adult physically prompting, you can use one of your own hands to prompt the pull of the child and the other hand to receive. Gradually, your outstretched hand, within a few inches of his, can replace the "hands on" prompt. When that is successful, the placement of your outstretched hand can be extended to one foot, three feet, six feet or across the room. The child's newly acquired communicative behavior will become embedded in his repertoire if he has numerous opportunities for repeated practice. As one initiating behavior begins to emerge, throughout the day concentrate on giving him a multitude of opportunities to practice before fading the prompts. Only after practice will he begin to initiate games with adults on his own.

Physical prompting can teach the child an acceptable way to communicate requests.

Physical prompts are gradually faded.

The use of photos to make a giggle game request can also be physically prompted, using two adults. Color photos of game props are highly effective. They should be 5 x 7 or 8 x 10, velcroed within easy reach and positioned at the eye-level of the child. Once again, the first adult *silently* moves behind the child, pushing him toward a photo of a favored game prop. He helps the child pick it up, walk over to the second adult and give it to the outstretched hand. The second adult points to the photo and exclaims "Want [*name of game*]?" several times as he takes the child over to the prop and begins the game.

Physically prompt a child to bring someone a game prop or a colored photo of a prop, or show him how to pull a person to a prop to initiate interaction.

If the child does not understand picture representation, the same procedure can be used with the prop itself. One adult helps the child pick up the prop and give it to the other adult. It is yet another way that initiation or requesting a giggle game can be shaped.

Practice all the ways a child can request an interaction. He will pick one that best suits him.

Once again, the key word to successful initiation is *practice*. Practice a variety of physical prompts with the child. It is unknown, at this time, which one the child will adopt to help get his needs met. Whether he chooses to bring a prop to an adult, bring a photo of the prop or pull an adult to the game, it serves the same purpose: to appropriately seek attention from another in requesting a favored giggle game.

Some day, he will reward your efforts by purposely seeking you out and initiating. It will be when you least expect it and will take you by surprise. In that one moment, your heart will fill with pride. You will know that you have given that child the gift of making an impact upon someone else in his life: to be active rather than passive and to develop a greater sense of who he is and what he is capable of doing.

LET'S IMAGINE

Example 1. Encourage initiation by physically prompting the child with two adults

EXAMPLE 1

The following example depicts how two adults can physically prompt a child to initiate a favored giggle game. The adult sees a student standing beside a tall file cabinet. This cabinet is used to hide behind in a "Peek-a-Boo" game.

PROBLEM

Jamaal establishes proximity to a favored game prop in order to initiate his favorite game. However, he does not direct communication to someone. If someone happens to see him by the prop, they play the game. There are times, however, when he is not noticed, leaves the area, and the teachable moment is lost.

SOLUTION

Monitor the child's actions closely and "catch" him by a game prop. Seize the moment and physically prompt the child from behind to seek out another adult to pull to the prop. This procedure trains initiation by showing the child that he can get an adult's hand, pull them to the prop, and then play a favored routine. Play the routine a few minutes and then have the second adult resume his prior activity nearby. Physically prompt the interaction again, fading the prompt a little more each time. Begin with a three to six-foot space between the child and retrieved adult so the child does not drop and tantrum when he is moved too far away from the prop. If the second adult is too far away initially, it will make it harder for the child to understand.

When the second adult is fairly close, and the child's hand is placed fairly quickly into his, the child will begin to understand the concept more readily and a behavior problem may not occur. Gradually widen the space between the child and second adult so that eventually he is pulling the second adult across the room to the prop.

PEEK-A-BOO

> One way a child can learn to initiate a favorite giggle game is by having one adult place the child's hand into another adult's hand. The adult helps the child pull the second adult to the desired game prop.

> The adult should be silent as he physically prompts the child. This allows the child to concentrate on the motor process involved rather than on the processing of auditory directions.

> After fading physical prompts, the second adult should remain nearby in case further physical prompting is necessary.

First adult:	*Physically prompts child around the corner of the cabinet from behind, over to second adult, three feet away.*
Child:	*Eye contact.*
First adult:	*Physically prompts child's hand to clasp second adult's outstretched hand.*
Child:	*Eye contact.*
First adult:	*Silently helps child "pull" second adult over to the cabinet.*
Child:	*Social smile.*
Second adult:	Peek-a-boo?
Child:	*Interest is shown by stillness of body and social smile.*
Second adult:	*Quickly positions himself around the other side of cabinet.* I...I...I...I'm... *with increased loudness (cue).*
Child:	G.
Second adult:	...going to get you! *Lunges from beside cabinet, picks up child and twirls him around (reinforcer).*
Child:	*Laughs.*

Second adult:	*Laughs, resumes another activity nearby.*
Child:	*Social smile, resumes original position beside cabinet.*
First adult:	*Resumes position of physically prompting child to retrieve second adult again.*

Continue physically prompting for ten minutes, widening the space between the child and the retrieved adult a little more each time.

LET'S IMAGINE

Example 2. Encouraging initiation by physically prompting the child by yourself

EXAMPLE 2

The following example depicts how one adult can physically prompt the child when there are not any other adults to aid the training of an initiation skill.

PROBLEM

Andrew does not yet initiate the "Rolling Ball" giggle game routine even though he loves it. Other adults are not available at this time to physically prompt the child to get the ball and bring it over.

SOLUTION

The solitary adult begins the familiar routine with the child and, after several repetitions, stops and extends her hand 6 inches from the child's hand. She gradually increases the distance between her extended hand and Andrew, beginning with 6 inches, then 1 foot, 3 feet, 6 feet, and then across the room. Each time the routine is ready to begin again, the adult increases the distance between her outstretched hand and the child. She continues to give him an expectant look. If the reinforcing turn is strong enough, he will eventually get up off the ball and walk across the room to the adult. The adult must then physically prompt his hand within hers and assume the body posture of him leading her back to the ball. This trains initiation by showing Andrew that he can take his partner's hand and pull her to the prop to begin a play routine.

ROLLING BALL

> One adult can successfully physically prompt a child to initiate a favored game.

> Prompting by one adult to aid the initiation of a game is achieved by standing near the game prop with an outstretched hand.

> Standing near the game prop with an outstretched hand provides the child with a visual cue of what is expected.

> The adult lightly "helps" the child place his hand in hers and then "helps" him pull her toward the game

Adult: *Positions child on his stomach on top of large ball and kneels in front, holding on to child's hands. This position maximizes eye contact.* Ball?

Child: *Eye contact.*

Adult: *Sings* Row, row, row the boat, gently down the stream. *Adult pulls the child by the hands back and forth on top of the ball.*

Child: *Social smile.*

Adult: Merrily, merrily, merrily, merrily.

Child: *Social smile.*

Adult: Life…is…but…a… (*cue*). *Continues to roll child back and forth but with a jerky movement accompanying each word.*

Child: Dream.

Adult: Dream! *Stops rolling, nuzzles chin into child's back.* (*reinforcer*).

Child: *Laughs.*

Adult: More? Ball? *Expectant look. Signs the word "more."*

Child: *Eye contact. Signs the word "more."*

Adult: More! *Keeps hand outstretched and with other hand places child's hand lightly within own outstretched hand, immediately beginning the routine again.*

Rolling Ball

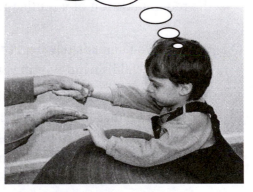

After the game has been repetitively played and the motivation is high, the adult signs and verbally prompts the word "more," attempting to move the child up the ladder of communication.

The adult lightly guides the child's hand, but she waits for him to complete the movement of placing his hand in hers.

WHAT? WHEN? WHY?

Answers to common questions

Q. How am I ever going to get the child to come across the room and pull me to a prop to initiate? Is there a way I can break down the teaching of this communication skill?

A. Yes, you can break it down into five objectives, and feel success with each tiny step. Structure the environment so the child is enabled to successfully "pull you" toward the game prop from six inches, one foot, three feet, six feet away, and from across the room. Begin with the first objective, physically prompting from six inches away. After several repetitions of the highly desired routine, stop and place your outstretched hand six inches away and say "More?" If the child does not take your hand to continue the interaction, physically prompt him to do so by placing your other hand upon his, pull him toward your outstretched hand and place his hand in yours. Say "More!', as if you now understand what he wants, and immediately begin the routine again. You are showing the child how to eventually lead you to the prop as well as how to continue the interaction when you move away slightly. Eventually, show the child how to lead you back to the prop from one foot away, three feet away, six feet away, and then from across the room. When the child is taking your hand and leading you to a prop from across the room, initiation of a routine is emerging.

Q. Why did you immediately begin the "Rolling Ball" routine again after you placed the child's hand within yours?

A. It is important to reinforce the child's action immediately so that he begins to understand that "if I place my hand in hers, the game will start again." If too much time elapses in between, the child may identify the beginning of the routine with a different stimulus and the wrong action might be reinforced.

Q. All of the physical prompting during a joint action routine seems to take a long time. Don't you lose the staying power of the child?

A. Actually, the opposite is true. Placing your hands on the child's hands and physically prompting through a turn helps him stay and focus. Also, in order to physically prompt him, the play space must be small, which aids staying power. Remember to have a strong reinforcing turn as well. Then he will be more apt to stay and "work" during his turn.

Q. How do you know when to fade the prompt?

A. You will know if you watch the child closely and *wait*. After several turns of prompting the child through his turn, begin to fade the prompt by offering 80 percent of your help and then 60, 40, 20 and 0 percent. Wait 5 to 10 seconds after you have helped him through 80 percent of the turn and look expectantly. If he doesn't follow through with the remaining 20 percent of the movement, prompt it for him several more times and then fade again.

Q. Why does the "first adult" silently physically prompt the child from behind?

A. It is important to eliminate distracting stimuli that the child may mistake as part of the whole or *gestalt* of the initiation process. By remaining quiet, the first adult is demonstrating to the child that body movement is the key element of this particular communicative act. This allows the child to concentrate on his movements instead of auditory processing the adult's directions.

Q. Why is it important for a child to learn how to initiate or request a giggle game routine?

A. Some children exhibit inappropriate behaviors for a variety of communicative reasons. Hitting, throwing, tantruming, pulling hair, screaming, pinching, scratching, or running out of the room may be a means by which a child may initiate interactions with others. If seeking interaction with/attention from others is one of the reasons for the inappropriate behavior, the behavior will begin to fade, for that reason, once the child is taught how to appropriately request a giggle game.

Q. I know a child that initiates giggle games with the adults in his life but not with other children. What can I do?

A. Use the same physical prompting techniques that were discussed in relation to adults. Instead of two adults, proceed with one adult and one peer or sibling.

OBJECTIVES WORKSHEET

After training initiation through physical prompts, the child initiates favorite giggle games

CHILD'S NAME_____

CURRENT LEVEL

This child waits for the adult to initiate an established giggle game. He does not yet take the adult's hand and lead her to game props. However, after this nonverbal communicative skill is established, he may be trained in how to give a photo of a game prop to an adult to make a request as well.

Date initiated_____ Date mastered_____

1. Given the child in proximity of the game prop and the adult three feet away, the child will take the adult's extended hand and pull her toward him, to initiate a giggle game. (This is a training phase.)

Date initiated_____ Date mastered_____

2. Given the child in proximity of the game prop and the adult six feet away, the child will take the adult's extended hand and pull her toward him, to initiate a giggle game. (This is a training phase.)

Date initiated_____ Date mastered_____

3. Given the child's desire to play a giggle game and the adult across the room, the child will walk over to the adult, take the adult's extended hand and pull her to the game prop, to initiate the game.

Date initiated_____ Date mastered_____

4. The child will initiate a favorite giggle game with an adult by giving the adult a photo of a game.

Date initiated_____ Date mastered_____

5. Given a child that has established proximity to a game prop or photo of a prop, he will allow physical prompting from behind by one adult to help engage another adult in play. (This child may tantrum, pull

away or drop when prompted, not understanding what is happening. Be careful to stage the entire prompting process between one to two feet so that he can quickly see what happens after the prompt.)

5

Verbal Play: Pre-Conversational Speech

CHAPTER OVERVIEW

In this chapter we will discuss what verbal play is and how to develop verbal play routines around the child's utterances. We will demonstrate how playing with words can develop social reciprocity, increase receptive and expressive language, and nurture the ability to stay on a topic. The specific format for developing verbal play during a giggle session will be broken down. Also, the five stages of verbal play will be discussed in detail, offering a multitude of examples and suggestions for successful implementation.

Dear Jacob,

Verbal play. Today we played with sounds as we imitated one another in glee. We have not yet played back and forth with words. It may come to pass some day and, then again, it may not. In the meantime, we will continue to playfully communicate with our hearts. It will be just as special; it's the language of love.

Love,

Miss Sue

Consider a child who is babbling, reproducing some sounds, makes funny, self-stimulatory sounds, and occasionally comes up with a word or a random sentence. There is some strength in this component part, even though it is not well developed. The key is to create a sense of intent around the component parts that are working.

Stanley I. Greenspan, *The Child with Special Needs*

WHAT IS VERBAL PLAY?

KEY POINTS

He's talking to an empty room? Choose one phrase and build a verbal game around it

The format for developing a verbal play routine is Imitate–Select–Model–Prompt.

As a child moves forward in his ability to initiate and maintain giggle time routines, he may acquire more language. Acquiring more language, however, does not necessarily mean that he has an understanding that words must be directed *to someone*. The room at large may be his conversational recipient and could very well be empty. Such a child can busy himself by talking to open spaces, reciting phrases from the television, or uttering a series of unrelated sentences. To add to the confusion, this verbiage often becomes one long bewildering monologue.

Even though echolalia serves a multitude of functions, he seems to have missed the seemingly obvious idea that language is a tool toward acquiring social connectedness with another. Specifically, how does one move a child who is shouting unrelated phrases toward an empty room closer to conversational speech? One way may be by incorporating all the principles learned thus far in giggle time and applying them to "verbal play." Following the child's lead, developing staying power, imitation, seizing the moment, verbal prompts, cueing, reinforcing turns,

Verbally imitate the child until you can select one of his random phrases and build a verbal play routine around it.

Develop a verbal routine with the child that involves changing one word of a selected phrase over and over again while remaining in one category.

Verbal play does not have to make sense. It is a time to "play" with words.

Verbal play works on the ability to stay on a topic by teaching the conceptual organizer of classification.

altering, waiting, repeating, utilizing props, movement, and rhyme are all utilized as well as one more principle: *following a topic.*

Working on the ability to stay on a topic involves developing joint action routines around the child's current language and, specifically, around one phrase. As the child randomly talks, the adult listens carefully for a phrase that could be used as the basis of a giggle time/verbal play routine. This phrase is selected from all the other utterances and becomes the main part of the verbal routine as it is broken down into several adult-and-child turns. From this phrase, the adult selects *one word* that can be constantly changed. It is exchanged for other words from the same category. This word that is constantly changed in the phrase is typically a noun or an adjective. For example, "Hey, let's go see <u>Sandy</u>" may become "Hey, let's go see <u>Lynn</u>," or "Hey, let's go see <u>AnnMarie</u>," or "Hey, let's go see <u>Tina</u>," as words are "flipped" through various proper names. The phrase "Her <u>elbows</u> were purple" might become "Her <u>legs</u> were purple," or "Her <u>hands</u> were purple," as words are "flipped" through the body part category.

When selecting a child's phrase to verbally play with, it is important to remember the primary goal: to connect with another through the playfulness of words. Remembering to stay playful is especially important when the adult imitates the child's verbiage and finds that the child's phrases do not make sense. For example, the child may say, "Eat a cow." Since it is "verbal play," it is OK to choose this phrase to build a routine around. The word "cow" could be changed to other farm animals as the child or adult says, "Eat a pig" or "Eat a horse." It is not the time to teach what we eat and don't eat. To do so would place the adult far above the child's level and staying power would be lost. Remember, the immediate goal is working on the ability to stay on a topic by teaching the concept of classification within a playful context — a context that is animated, motivational, and nonsensical, yet highly instructional.

In the verbal play procedure, the adult verbally imitates the child until the child says a single word or phrase that depicts a category. Then the adult and child develop a short routine around it, "flipping" one word of the phrase back and forth while remaining in that category. As this is done, the child learns how to stay on a topic as he searches for words within that classification. The child's flurry of unrelated phrases will stop momentarily as he joins the adult in passing the "flipped" word and patterned phrase back and forth.

The problem is getting the child to "flip" a category back and forth. There are four words that will aid the adult in remembering how to successfully move the child toward this goal. The four words are *Imitate–Select–Model–Prompt*. As the adult moves through the sequence of these four words, the verbal play routine will be a successful endeavor.

In summary, *verbally imitate* the child until one phrase or single word is *selected*, *model* the "flipping" of one word from that phrase on your next three turns, *verbally prompt* three more words in a row from the category with a questioning tone and wait expectantly. When the child finally states one of the prompted words or retrieves a new word from the category, repeat what he said, pair it with a *cue* and quickly do a *reinforcing turn*. The verbal play pattern has now emerged.

Begin again and refine the beginning turns of the routine as needed by adding movement and sounds for interest. Through verbal play, the child will learn about conversations. He will find that conversations are made up of words that connect people and center around one topic for a period of time before moving on. Conversations can be fun and playful, an avenue of mutual enjoyment. Through verbal play he may learn how to connect, play, and stay.

> *Conversational flow develops after the child demonstrates an understanding of the verbal play pattern by easily "flipping" a modeled, prompted or novel word from the category on his turn and continues the verbal play routine with the adult for ten minutes.*

> *After the child demonstrates an understanding by "flipping" a modeled, prompted or novel word from the category on his turn, it is time to add a cue and an ending reinforcing turn to complete the verbal routine.*

The four word "verbal play" format:
Imitate–Select–Model–Prompt

1. *Listen to the child's unrelated words and sentences and verbally imitate until one phrase or word conducive to building a verbal play pattern is selected.*

2. *Using a questioning reflection, repeat the selected word/phrase back to the child.*

3. *Wait for the child's turn. It may be eye contact, social smile, movement or verbalization.*

4. *Repeat the word/phrase again, this time modeling for the first time how to "flip" to another word in that category.*

5. *Wait for a turn from the child.*

6. *Model how to "flip" another word from the category for the second time.*

7. *Wait for a turn from the child.*

8. *Model how to "flip" another word from the category for the third time.*

9. *Wait for a turn from the child.*

10. *State the phrase again and verbally prompt three more words in a row from the category using a questioning tone.*

11. *Wait for his turn.*

12. *If he "takes the bait" and repeats one of the prompted words, repeat what he said, adding a cue and reinforcer. This will end the sequence. Begin the routine again with the chosen phrase.*

LET'S IMAGINE

How to develop verbal play routines by following the verbal play format: Imitate–Select–Model–Prompt

EXAMPLE

The following example demonstrates the *verbal play format: Imitate–Select–Model–Prompt*. The adult continues the format over and over until the child demonstrates an understanding of an emerging word pattern by stating either a modeled or prompted word on her turn.

PROBLEM

Rose has very little staying power. Typically, she directs unrelated sentences toward empty rooms. Sentences are delayed echolalia of conversations and television shows.

SOLUTION

The play space is small, one foot. Rose is sitting, face to face, on the adult's lap. The adult begins by imitating Rose and listening for a phrase around which a verbal routine can be built. As Rose continually changes phrases, the adult follows her lead by continuing to imitate her. The adult continues to *imitate* Rose's phrases until a new phrase is *selected*. Then the adult begins the *modeling* and *prompting* phase of the *verbal play format* as she attempts to build a verbal play routine with Rose.

MARY'S LITTLE DUCK

During verbal play, some of the child's turns are verbal and some are nonverbal.

In this verbal play example, the adult selected the phrase "wiggle the joy stick, Bert" and the word "Bert" was chosen to flip through the proper name category. The adult modeled and prompted names of familiar classmates and family members.

Child: And while you guys are wiggling the joy stick, I will sing you a little song about what you're doing, OK? *Child is on adult's lap but head is turned and eye gaze and verbalizations are directed away from the adult.*

Adult: Wiggling the joy stick? (*Imitate.*)

Child: Let me see here. Let's look at this. It's on the top and you're supposed to wiggle the joy stick, <u>Bert</u> (*select*). *The adult selects this phrase and the word "Bert" in the phrase to flip in the proper name category. Names of familiar classmates and family members will be modeled and prompted.*

Adult: And you're supposed to wiggle the joy stick, <u>Tommy</u> (*first model*).

Child: *Silence. Sitting very still. One-second eye gaze. Nonverbal turn.*

Adult: And you're supposed to wiggle the joy stick, <u>Kevin</u> (*second model*). *Adult wiggles his body back and forth as the word "wiggle" is said. Added movement for interest and the promotion of staying power.*

Child: *Social smile, looking down. Nonverbal turn.*

Adult: And you're supposed to wiggle the joy stick, <u>Patric</u> (*third model*). *Continues flipping the proper name word and repeating this phrase since the child appears interested. Continues to wiggle his body each time wiggle is said.*

Child: *Glance, social smile.*

Adult: And you're supposed to wiggle the joy stick, <u>Brooke</u>, <u>Jacob</u>, <u>Ryan</u>? (*Prompt.*) *Prompting is done with heavy inflection as if adult expects an answer. It must become clear to the child, through verbal prompting, what is expected.*

When the child did not continue the word pattern by following the modeled or prompted words, the adult continued to imitate until a new phrase was selected.

Child: Old Macdonald's farm.

Adult: Old Macdonald's farm (*imitate*). *The prompting of names did not work. The child did not choose one to complete the emerging pattern on her turn. The adult begins verbal imitation again. Adult listens for a new phrase to select and follows verbal lead.*

Child: On his farm he had a chick. EIEIO.

Adult: On his farm he had a chick. EIEIO (*imitate*). *Adult isn't sure that child knows farm animals so does not pick a word from this phrase.*

Once again, a new phrase was selected and the adult modeled and prompted again. However, the child still did not respond, on her turn, with a modeled or prompted word, so imitation of the child's phrases began for the third time.

Child: On his farm he had a chick. EIEIO.

Adult: EIEI<u>O</u> (*select*). *Adult knows the child loves the alphabet and chooses this phrase and the alphabet category, attempting a verbal play routine once again.*

Child: *Quick turn of head toward adult.*

Adult: EIEI<u>S</u> (*first model*). *The child's hands are taken into the adult's and his upper body is moved back and forth to the tempo of "EIEIS."*

Child: *Glance.*

Adult: EIEI<u>I</u> (*second model*). *The child's hands are taken into the adult's and his upper body is moved back and forth to the tempo of "EIEIJ," for interest.*

Child: *Social smile.*

Adult: EIEI<u>W</u> (*third model*). *The child's hands are taken into the adult's and his upper body is moved back and forth to the tempo of "EIEIW."*

Child: *Social smile.*

> In verbal play, follow the child's verbal lead when necessary, but continue to strive toward staying in one category.

Adult: EIEI <u>C</u>…<u>V</u>…<u>W</u>? (*Prompt.*) *Prompting is done, once again, with heavy inflection as if an answer is expected. It must become clear to the child, through verbal prompting, what is expected.*

Child: Shoes off kind.

> If it is too difficult to imitate a child's long sentence during the imitation phase of the verbal phase format, imitate just a part of it.

Adult: Shoes off kind (*imitate*). *Prompting of alphabet letters didn't work so begin verbal imitation again. Adult is on look-out for a new phrase to select. Follows verbal lead.*

Child: Mary's little duck…

Adult: Mary's little duck… (*Imitate.*)

Child: and his elbows were purple.

Adult: Mary's little duck and his elbows were <u>purple</u> (*select*). *Adds movement by bouncing child on lap with each word recited. Picks colors to "flip" since child knows his colors. If color category doesn't work, body parts could be attempted, flipping the word "elbow."*

Child: *Eye contact.*

Adult: Mary's little duck and his elbows were <u>orange</u> (*first model*). *Continues bouncing movement.*

Child: *Eye contact.*

Adult: Mary's little duck and his elbows were <u>green</u> (*second model*). *Continues bouncing movement.*

Child: *Eye contact.*

Adult: Mary's little duck and his elbows were <u>red</u> (*third model*). *Continues bouncing movement.*

Child: *Social smile.*

Adult: Mary's little duck and his elbows were <u>blue</u>... <u>brown</u>...<u>yellow</u>? (*Prompt.*) *Prompting is done, once again, with heavy inflection as if adult expects an answer. It must become clear to the child, through verbal prompting, what is expected of him.*

Child: <u>Purple</u>. *Child doesn't take the prompt but is beginning to understand that the adult has keyed in on the color. He stayed on same topic, did not change the phrase.*

Adult: Mary's little duck and his elbows were <u>black</u> (*model again*). *Continues bouncing to each word. Adult attempts a model, staying on topic of color.*

Child: *Eye contact.*

Adult: Mary's little duck and his elbows were <u>pink</u> (*model again*). *Continues bouncing to each word. Adult attempts a model, staying on topic of color.*

Child: *Eye contact.*

Adult: Mary's little duck and his elbows were <u>white</u> (*model again*). *Continues bouncing to each word. Adult attempts a model, staying on topic of color.*

Child: *Eye contact.*

Adult: Mary's little duck and his elbows were <u>orange</u>, <u>green</u>, <u>red</u>? (*Prompt again.*) *Adult looks expectantly, hoping child will say a modeled or prompted color word.*

Child: <u>Red</u>.

Adult: <u>Red</u>! *Hooray, hooray! He understands that we are staying on the topic of color! He chose a prompted word so we now have the "core" of the routine. It's time to start thinking of a reinforcing turn. Shakes child quickly back and forth on lap. Adult sees if he likes this movement. If he does, it can be the reinforcing turn. If not, may attempt to flip him backwards off the lap, a tickle, or a large circular movement might be tried.*

Child: *Sustained eye contact. Laugh.*

Adult: *Yea! He liked the shake! Now the "core" of the verbal play routine has been established. The shake will be the reinforcer, color words will be the "flipped" category, and the adult's turn prior to the reinforcing turn can be cued.* Mary's little duck and his elbows – *"Core" of verbal routine begins. Bounces child on lap to the beat.*

Child: *Eye contact.*

Adult: w...e...r...e... *Whispered slowly. Rising inflection on word "were" for increased anticipation (cue).*

Child: <u>Green</u>.

Adult: <u>Green</u>! *Said loudly with animation. Shakes child quickly back and forth as the word is repeated (reinforcer).*

Child: *Laughs.*

Repeat the core of the verbal play sequence, using different color words, for ten minutes.

WHAT? WHEN? WHY?

Answers to common questions

Q. What is the goal of patterned verbal play?

A. The primary goal is the child's independent retrieval of words in a category on his turn.

Q. Why is it important for the child to master patterned verbal play?

A. This skill increases expressive language as well as the ability to stay on one topic or category for a sustained period of time. In order to be successful in conversational speech, the child must understand that sentences between two partners are connected by a topic or theme. Conversational flow develops when one partner's utterances are related to the utterances of the other.

Q. Can you explain again how to make verbal play out of a child's phrase?

A. Select one word from his phrase and keep changing that particular word each time the phrase is recited. For example, in the phrase "Let's go see <u>Sue</u>," proper names of people would be changed or "flipped." Names of people he is familiar with would be modeled and prompted. In the phrase, "Let's eat a <u>tiger</u>," zoo animal names would be changed or "flipped."

Q. What do you mean by "flipping" a word of a phrase?

A. When I talk of "flipping" a word, I visualize a deck of cards, each with a different word on it from one category of words. Each time the phrase is spoken, a new word card is "flipped" in my mind and inserted into the phrase.

Q. How can I be sure that I am choosing the right phrase to build a verbal routine around? He says so many phrases!

A. Listen for a category in a phrase that may be familiar to the child. The words that you will both be "flipping" through should be from a category that he is receptively and expressively familiar with. If he does not know his colors, numbers, or names of foods, you would not choose a word in these categories from any of his phrases. Think about the child's favorite songs or giggle games. Perhaps he is familiar with categories embedded within them. If you know that he has the expressive language to retrieve farm animals, numbers, colors or letters, a phrase including one of these categories might work. You will never be sure. Follow his lead and keep trying. In the meantime, you are building staying power.

Q. What else do I do while I am imitating and listening for a possible phrase?

A. Wait, wait, and wait some more for a phrase that might work. It's similar to a game of jump rope. If two people are swinging a jump rope and you leap into the rope too soon or too late, you will become entangled. When this happens, you must jump out, wait, and jump in again. It's the same in verbal play. If you jump into a phrase, flip a word and it doesn't work, then get out. Listen, imitate, and be ready to select and jump into a different phrase. As the child continues to talk there will be other phrases to try.

Q. What if you are flipping words in the farm category and he suddenly says a zoo animal on his turn?

A. Follow his lead and begin modeling and prompting the new classification, zoo animals. Signal the change of category by prefacing your turn with "Zoo?'

Q. You said, "As the child talks, listen for a word or a phrase to use as a topic." What if the child does not speak in phrases but in single words? Do you mean that a topic can be built around a single word instead of a phrase?

A. Yes. Some children have mastered joint action routines, display adequate staying power but are at an emergent language stage. They do not yet speak in phrases or sentences but with single words. They are prime candidates for single-word verbal play. Others may simply not respond to a routine being built around a phrase. Their staying power may be very short and when you recite a long phrase on your turn it may take too long. They may lose interest and the moment will be lost. These particular children respond better when a verbal routine is played at a much faster pace. This is possible with single-word verbal play. An example of single-word verbal play is in the next section, "Verbal play: stages 1 to 5."

Q. What is verbal prompting?

A. After the adult has modeled three examples of flipping the word in the category, he verbally prompts the child by saying three words in a row that the child could say on his turn. It needs to be done with a heavy questioning inflection and exaggerated expression. Its tone sounds different from the other adult turns. This difference cues the child that something is expected of him.

Q. What if the child perseverates, continually repeating the original phrase on his turn without flipping the category?

A. Continue modeling what you want him to do when it is your turn. On each of your turns, flip to a new word in the category, using the same phrase each time.

Q. When do you stop using the verbal play format of Imitate–Select–Model–Prompt and move into the flow or "core" of the verbal routine?

A. As soon as the child understands that one word is being flipped in a category, and does so on his turn, the verbal play format of Imitate–Select–Model–Prompt can be dropped. The child's understanding will be evident when you have modeled and prompted several adult turns and the child states one of the modeled or prompted words on his turn. Once this happens, the verbal play format is dropped and the routine will begin to flow smoothly. The adult will continue to stop momentarily each time she gets to the "flipped" word but the child will begin to fill in a word from the category with fun and ease as he repetitively plays his turns in the sequence.

Q. After you stop using the verbal play format, what do you do?

A. Add a cue and a reinforcing turn to complete the sequence and then repetitively play it for ten minutes.

Q. What if the child doesn't use one of my modeled or prompted words, but retrieves one of his own from the desired category?

A. This is the ultimate goal! To do so would mean that he thoroughly understands how to stay in a category and rotate through it on his turn. He would be actively playing with you, manipulating words between the two of you for enjoyment. This is a higher level, which usually comes with time.

OBJECTIVES WORKSHEET

Implement the verbal play format of Imitate–Select–Model–Prompt into an interaction

CHILD'S NAME _____

CURRENT LEVEL

This child does not yet understand that language is supposed to be directed to someone. He does use words to socially connect with another in a reciprocal manner. When speaking, he does not relate his sentences to his partners and stay on a topic.

Date initiated_____ Date mastered_____

1. Given the verbal play format of Imitate–Select–Model–Prompt, the child will state one of the adult's modeled or prompted words to maintain the interaction.

Date initiated_____ Date mastered_____

2. Given the verbal play format of Imitate–Select–Model–Prompt, the child will maintain the interaction by generating a new word in the classification on his turn.

Date initiated_____ Date mastered_____

3. Given a verbal play routine, the child will remain engaged with the adult for ten minutes.

...perhaps joy can be practiced. Perhaps we can decide to be happy, to give joy before waiting to receive it. This is not denial but affirmation of the power inside us... Then we become the ones who teach the meaning of joy to our children, as well as allowing them to teach it to us.

Marrianne Williamson, *A Womans Worth*

VERBAL PLAY – STAGES 1 TO 5

KEY POINTS

How can I verbally play with one child who uses single words and sounds and another child who speaks in sentences?

> There appear to be five stages that some children move through while developing verbal play.

> The language in each stage progresses in complexity.

> Verbal play appears to be a vehicle toward conversational speech for some children.

> Stage 1 strives to increase the child's vocalizations.

Some children appear to move through a sequence of five "verbal stages" while developing "verbal play" skills. The language in each stage progressively becoming more complex. In overview, verbal play stage 1 involves a mixture of physical and verbal imitation. Verbal play stages 2 and 3 involve single-word play and contains a physical component. Touch and/or movement are the reinforcers and are necessary in these early stages. Stage 4 incorporates phrases and sentences into the play. Movement and touch may not be as necessary since playing with language is reinforcing for the child now. Stage 5 is prompted conversational speech.

Verbal play stage 1 is verbal and physical imitation, no topic. In stage 1, the child is making sounds, saying words and/or phrases and moving his body all at the same time. At this stage, the goal is for the child to develop staying power as well as increase his verbalizations. "Children tend to do more of the behavior that adults attend to; less of the behaviors adults ignore" (MacDonald 1998). Thus, repeating a child's vocalizations back to him will increase his vocalizations. As the child is imitated precisely, he will delight the adult with a steady conversational flow of

Stage 2 strives to assign meaning to the child's random sounds.

movement, sounds, babbling, facial expressions, single words, and phrases.

Verbal play stage 2 is single words and sounds, random topics. Stage 2 consists of an odd mixture of topics, sounds and single words. The adult begins to assign meaning to the child's sounds by interpreting the sounds as word approximations from categories. Single words, from many categories, are tossed back and forth between the adult and child. Play with words is the primary goal of this early stage. Incorporating movement, touch, a cue and reinforcing turn into the verbal play is imperative.

As the play progresses to verbal play stage 3, sounds are dropped and single words on one topic develop. Single-word play revolves around one category or classification. Movement and touch continue to be primary components as well as a cue and reinforcing turn. Eventually, in verbal play stage 4, movement/touch may be dropped as single words on a topic expand to phrases and sentences in one topic area. This stage is called "phrases and sentences on one topic." A cue and reinforcing turn are now optional. They are only added if staying power is weak and the play with language is not yet reinforcing in and of itself.

Stages 3, 4 and 5 strive to remain in one classification area or on one topic.

In verbal play stage 5, the child begins to move toward conversational speech with the aid of verbal prompts. This fifth stage is called prompted conversational speech on one familiar topic. The child, while conversing with the primary adult partner, is softly verbally prompted from behind by a second adult.

When prompting conversational speech in stage 5, a topic with familiar vocabulary is chosen and the conversation makes sense.

The primary partner chooses a topic that is familiar to the child. This way, the vocabulary is familiar and less prompting is necessary. Vocabulary from a previous giggle game or familiar song might be introduced as a topic. For example, the child may be able to converse about "emotions" because of the song "If you're happy and you know it." Or, verbal play about animals might emerge because of the child's prior knowledge of animal names from "Old Macdonald" and "Down on Grandpa's farm."

During this last stage, a cue and reinforcing turn are not used. The adult, the conversation itself and the connection between the partners become the reinforcers for the child.

LET'S IMAGINE: VERBAL PLAY STAGE 1

Verbal and physical imitation, no topic

EXAMPLE

In the following example, the adult and child stay within a small play space of one foot. The child's turns are made up of single words, phrases, body movements, facial expressions and babbling.

PROBLEM

Dominic moves quickly through a combination of sounds, movements and unconnected phrases, mixing them all together into one long exchange. He enjoys the interaction with an adult but staying power is still quite weak. He may initiate interaction through negative behaviors as well.

SOLUTION

The adult's turns are imitation with the exception of adding a sound or word to a child's turn of movement. This adds interest, staying power and focused attention. Playing with lots of words becomes the priority, regardless of content. The adult's facial expressions must also be dramatic and exaggerated. The only portion of the verbal play format that is implemented in stage 1 is imitation.

FOLLOW LEAD

Child: *Blows kiss with hand on mouth. Action only.*

Adult: *Blows kiss with hand on mouth. Adds a sound to the child's previous action by smacking lips as blows a kiss in imitation.* Mmmmm.

Child: Oo, oo, oo!

Adult: Oo, oo, oo! (*Imitation*)

In stage 1 of verbal play, the entire format of Imitate–Select–Model–Prompt is not used. The adult utilizes an abbreviated format consisting only of imitation, the purpose of which is to increase verbal and non-verbal turns.

Stage 1 of verbal play is a combination of verbal and nonverbal turns.

In stage 1, a cue and reinforcing turn are not played.

Child: Sit down chair!

Adult: Sit down chair!

Child: *Laugh.*

Adult: *Laugh.*

Child: *Presses on each nail of adult's hand. Action only.*

Adult: *Says* ouch *each time a nail is pushed, adding sound to action.*

Child: Osh osh b gosh.

Adult: Osh osh b gosh.

Child: Be nice.

Adult: Be nice.

Child: *Opens mouth, tongue out.*

Adult: *Opens mouth, tongue out.*

Child: Goofy! *Giggles, wrinkles nose.*

Adult: Goofy! *Giggles, wrinkles nose.*

Child: No, no, goo.

Adult: No, no, goo.

Child: *Lies on floor, hides face.*

Adult: *Lies on floor, hides face, adds snoring sound.*

Continues for ten minutes.

LET'S IMAGINE: VERBAL PLAY STAGE 2

Single words and sounds, random topics

EXAMPLE

In the following example, the adult observes Michael vocalizing. She seizes the moment and attempts to create a verbal game out of his word approximations and sounds. This is different than verbal play stage 1 in which the adult simply imitates the child's vocalizations without the intention of developing a topic routine. In stage 2 the objective is to simply assign meaning to the child's sounds. She attempts to assign meaning in particular classification areas, introducing the idea of staying on a topic.

PROBLEM

Michael's spontaneous speech is emerging, unclear and approximated. He says many unrelated words, mixed together with sounds. He plays an assortment of giggle games and displays adequate staying power but does not yet stay on one topic or in one classification area. His turns are still unrelated to the verbal turns of the adult.

SOLUTION

Michael does not yet understand how to stay on a topic so as he utters a variety of sounds, a variety of topics are introduced. A variety is introduced because the adult listens closely to the sounds and word approximations offered by Michael on his turn. If the adult can assign meaning to one of his sounds by switching to a new category, she must do so since the main purpose is to give meaning to sounds and word approximations. For example, in the following routine, the adult hears a sound that might be interpreted as a vehicle sound. She proceeds to give meaning to Michael's sounds in the transportation category until she hears a vocalization that she cannot assign a vehicle sound to. She hears, instead, something that might be interpreted as an animal sound, so she moves into the animal category. The example begins in the category of transportation and then moves to the farm animal category, following Michael's lead of sounds and approximations. As the adult searches for categorical nouns or verbs that she can assign to his vocalizations, she retrieves words from songs that he has heard repeatedly throughout the day in songs or videos. This ensures his interest and receptive language of the categories introduced. In the following example the *cue* is a startled look on the part of the adult prior to wiggling a body part. The *reinforcer* is the actual wiggling of the body part. The verbal play format of Select–Imitate–Model–Prompt is implemented in verbal play stage 2.

TRANSPORTATION AND PETS

> Adult continues to follow child's lead, listening to his sounds/words and attaching meaning to them.

Child: *Touches his ear while making eye contact.* Eeee.

Adult: *Startled look. Touches child's ear.* Eeee? (*Imitate.*)

Child: *Social smile.*

Adult: *Wiggles child's ears.* <u>Car</u>, beep-beep? *(Select.)* (*First model.*) *Adult selects the "Eeee" sound and gives meaning to it by changing it to "beep."*

Child: *Laughs.* Bee, bee.

Throughout the stage 2 example, the cue is the adult's startled look and the reinforcer is wiggling the child.

Since the child's spontaneous speech is emerging, unclear and approximated, the adult continues to search for sounds and words that are similar to his vocalizations.

The adult then gives meaning to the approximations by changing the category if the child's sound or word approximation warrants it.

The child doesn't really have an understanding of categories at this point. He is imitating the adult's sounds on most of his turns.

Imitation, developing staying power, manipulating sounds, enjoying the interaction with another and strengthening receptive language are adequate goals for this stage.

Imitate–Select–Model is implemented in stage 2 of verbal play. Prompting the child in the category may also be tried in this early stage.

Adult: *Startled look.*

Child: *Social smile.*

Adult: *Wiggles child's nose.* <u>Train</u>, choo-choo *(second model)*.

Child: *Laughs.* Oo-Oo.

Adult: *Startled look.*

Child: *Social smile.*

Adult: *Wiggles child's tummy,* <u>Fire engine</u>, errrrrrr *(third model)*.

Child: *Laughs.* Oy.

Adult: *Startled look. The adult can't think of a vehicle that makes this sound so she switches to farm category.*

Child: *Social smile.*

Adult: *Wiggles child's knees.* <u>Pig</u>, oink, oink? *(Select again.) (First model.) Adult gives meaning to "oy" sound by saying* oink, oink.

Child: *Laughs.* Oyk.

Adult: *Startled look.*

Child: *Social smile.*

Adult: *Wiggles child's feet.* <u>Chicken</u>, cluck, cluck *(second model)*.

Child: *Laughs.* Uck.

Adult: *Startled look.*

Child: *Social smile.*

Adult: *Wiggles child's hands.* <u>Cow</u>, moo, moo *(third model)*.

Child: *Laughs.* Oo.

Continue assigning meaning to sounds and words for ten minutes.

LET'S IMAGINE: VERBAL PLAY STAGE 3

Single words on one topic

EXAMPLE

In the following example, Sarah is eating lunch. She looks over at the adult and smiles as she takes a bite of cookie. The adult attempts to build a verbal play routine by "flipping" single words in the food category. The goal is for Sarah to play with language as well as stay on one topic.

PROBLEM

Sarah's receptive language is stronger than her expressive language. She loves to interact with adults but, when interacting, uses unrelated single words.

SOLUTION

Since Sarah enjoys many kinds of foods and her receptive language is strong in this area, a verbal play game is attempted around this topic. Lunchtime is chosen as an opportunity to develop this game since visual cues of various foods are within view to aid her word retrieval. The verbal play format of Imitate–Select–Model–Prompt is utilized in verbal play stage 3.

FOOD

The verbal play format of Imitate–Select–Model–Prompt is utilized in stage 3 of verbal play.

Once the verbal play routine is developed, the verbal play format of Imitate–Select–Model–Prompt can be dropped since the child understands how to stay on the topic when it is his turn.

Adult: What is that?

Child: Cookie.

Adult: <u>Cookie</u>! (*Imitate.*) (*Select.*)

Child: Cookie!

Adult: <u>Hotdog</u>! (*First model.*)

Child: Cookie!

Adult: <u>Hamburger</u>! (*Second model.*)

Child: Cookie!

Adult: <u>French fries</u>! (*Third model.*)

Child: Cookie!

Adult: <u>Sandwich</u>…<u>candy</u>…<u>pizza</u>? *The adult slowly prompts three words from the food category. Then on the word "pizza," uses a rising inflection and an*

> The cue and reinforcing turn will remain the same throughout the ten-minute interaction.

> When verbally prompting three possible words from a category, use an expectant look and a questioning inflection to visually and auditorily cue the child that he is expected to respond.

expectant look, as though she expects a response (*prompt*).

Child: <u>Pizza</u>! *Sarah displays understanding of verbal play by stating a prompted word. The remainder of the verbal routine, or core, will now be refined and a cue and reinforcer added. Then it will be repetitively played.*

Adult: <u>PIZZA</u>! (*Cue.*) *The adult added a cue by shouting the word.*

Child: *Eye contact, social smile.*

Adult: Oh no! *Picks up child under arms and twirls him around* (*reinforcer*).

Child: *Laughs.*

Routine continues for ten minutes with names of other favorite foods tossed back and forth.

LET'S IMAGINE: VERBAL PLAY STAGE 4

Phrases and sentences on one topic

EXAMPLE

In the following example, Terry shows an adult a pencil. It has a cube on top of it, each side depicting a different face. The adult must be careful not to ask the typical questions; "What is that? Where did you get it? Who gave it to you?" These questions are above Terry's level of language at this time.

PROBLEM

Terry's staying power is adequate. He plays many giggle games with a variety of adults. His expressive language is limited. Word retrieval is difficult. He is eager to relate to the adults in his life; however, his phrases and sentences are unrelated and intermingled with many subtle nonverbal turns. He often gives up in his communicative attempts to share information and walks away, especially if the adult poses questions that are too difficult for him to respond to.

SOLUTION

It's important to respond to Terry's communicative attempts at his level while building his skills and showing him how to stay on a topic. This is done by developing a verbal play game around a familiar topic. The adult moves Terry toward the topic of "emotion" through modeling and prompting. This topic is chosen because he is familiar with the "emotion" vocabulary from the song "If you're happy and you know it." The song is a favorite of his and depicts various emotions in its lyrics. The adult is careful to acknowledge Terry's subtle nonverbal turns as well, giving meaning to them by responding with an adult turn. The adult also remembers that this is verbal *play* and the routine that develops does not have to "make sense."

HAPPY NEW YEAR

> Be careful, do not ask typical questions in verbal play. Instead of asking a question, imitate. It will give you some time to think of your next turn.

> Intersperse exaggerated movements and drama into the verbal play routine for interest.

Child: *Terry points to the top of the pencil where the faces are, displaying a nonverbal turn of pointing to the pencil.*

Adult: What does he say? *Adult points to one of the faces on the pencil.*

Child: Happy New Year!

Adult: He s…a…y…s…Happy New Year? (*Imitate.*) *Adult throws her arms into the air and waves her hands back and forth with great exaggeration to sustain interest . Adult hears Terry say "Happy New Year" and must quickly decide if there is a word in the phrase that can be "flipped" through a category. Adult decides on the category of emotions (select).*

Child: *Laughs, throws his arms into the air and waves his hands also, displaying a nonverbal turn.*

Adult: *Turns the pencil and points to the next face with an expectant look.* He s…a…y…s…Sad New Year! *Waves arms and hands in the air (first model).*

Child: *Imitates adult's body movement, nonverbal turn. Laughs, throws his arms up and waves hands in the air.*

Adult: *Turns the pencil and points to the next face with an expectant look.* He s…a…y…s…Silly New Year! *Waves arms and hands in the air (second model).*

Child: *Imitates adult's body movement, nonverbal turn. Laughs and throws his arms up and waves hands in the air.*

Adult: *Turns the pencil and points to the next face with an expectant look.* He s…a…y…s…<u>Mad</u> New Year! *Waves arms and hands in the air (third model).*

Child: *Imitates adult's body movement, nonverbal turn. Laughs and throws his arms up and waves hands in the air.*

Adult: *Turns the pencil and points to the next face with an expectant look.* He s…a…y…s…<u>Sad</u>?, <u>Happy</u>?, <u>Excited</u>? *(Prompt.) The adult prompts three emotion words for the child. The rising inflection indicates to the child that he is supposed to choose one.*

Child: <u>Excited!</u>

Adult: He s…a…y…s… *(cue),* <u>Excited</u> New Year! *Adult repeats what the child said, adding a cue. The child has chosen one of the three words and needs to be reinforced. The child has been enjoying the exaggerated waving of the adult's arms and hands so this can remain in the sequence (reinforcer.)*

Child: *Laughs, throws his arms and hands up in the air. He imitates the adult's movement.*

Adult: *Begins to repetitively play the "core" or remainder of the routine. Adult turns the pencil and points to the next face with an expectant look.* He s…a…y…s… *Adult waits expectantly, not modeling or prompting right away.*

Child: He says, <u>Silly</u> New Year! *Waiting worked! He states an emotion word from one modeled previously! This demonstrates his understanding of which word is being flipped. He is also staying on the topic of emotion.*

Adult: He s…a…y…s… *(cue),* <u>Silly</u> New Year! *Repeats what the child said. Waves arms and hands in the air (reinforcer).*

> *Use the verbal play format of Imitate–Select–Model–Prompt in stage 4 until the verbal pattern is developed, then add a cue and reinforcing turn.*

Child: *Laughs, throws his arms and hands up in the air.*

The verbal play routine continues with the adult beginning the sequence again. "Silly," "Grumpy," and "Scared" are additional words that are played in the next ten minutes of interaction.

LET'S IMAGINE: VERBAL PLAY STAGE 5

Prompted conversational speech on one familiar topic that includes two adults, no movement, cue or reinforcer

EXAMPLE

In the following example, Jessica has easily "flipped" the food category in other verbal play routines. An attempt will now be made to engage her in conversational speech about her favorite foods.

PROBLEM

Jessica now engages in a variety of verbal play routines, staying on the topic and flipping words in specific categories with fun and ease. However, when conversational speech is initiated by an adult, she is unable to answer and remains silent. She often turns her head away in response.

SOLUTION

Jessica is verbally prompted by a second adult in the beginning of the following conversation and then the prompts gradually fade. The child stands between the two adults, the first adult being the conversationalist and the second adult the prompter. The second adult prompts the child by *whispering* appropriate responses in Jessica's ear. However, he *waits* to prompt, giving the child adequate time to process the information.

FOODS AT HOME

> Choose a topic that is very familiar to the child.

Adult: What do you like to eat? *The child is within one foot of the adults.*

Child: Banana. *Verbal prompt is whispered in ear by second adult.*

Adult: Banana! What else do you like to eat?

Child: Ice cream. *Verbal prompt by second adult.*

Adult: Oh, me too. I love ice cream. What else?

Child: Ummm, tuna fish. *No prompt needed, independent response.*

Verbal prompting by the second adult gradually fades.

Adult: Tuna fish tastes good! Do you like apples?

Child: Yes. *Verbal prompt by second adult.*

Adult: Do you like peanut butter and jelly?

Child: Yes. *Verbal prompt by second adult.*

Adult: What else?

Child: Sandwich and cookie.

Adult: Sandwich and cookie? What else?

Child: Cookies up there.

Verbal prompting must be done discreetly by whispering in the child's ear. It must appear very different from the conversational tone used by the first adult.

Adult: The cookies are up high on the shelf?

Child: Yes. *Verbal prompt by second adult.*

Adult: Do you eat hotdogs?

Child: Somedays I eat a hotdog.

Adult: Yeah, me too. Somedays. What else do you eat somedays?

Child: Somedays I eat candy.

Adult: Hmm, that tastes good! What do you eat for breakfast?

Child: Cereal. *Verbal prompt from second adult is needed again.*

Adult: Cereal?

Child: Yes, cereal bars! *No prompt is needed.*

Adult: Yum! Cereal bars are good!

Child: I eat blueberry and strawberry and apple cinnamon bars! *No prompt is needed. Note that the child's spontaneous sentences are getting longer. These are favorite foods and she hears the language daily.*

Adult: Oh…that's good stuff, isn't it?

Child: That's good stuff! *No prompt is needed. In a conversation, the sentences flow with one leading into the next. She is beginning to understand this. She often repeats portions of the adult's previous sentence or adds to it.*

The conversation surrounding food is continued for another five minutes, with prompting by the second adult as needed.

WHAT? WHEN? WHY?

_____

Answers to common questions

Q. I'm confused. I thought all of the child's turns in verbal play would be verbal?

A. Actually, only one of the child's turns needs to be verbal, the "flipped" word. Since the ability to stay on one topic is being developed, this is the most important turn that the child engages in.

Q. Why do you choose a topic that has already been a verbal play game when prompting conversational speech in stage 5?

A. The child is familiar with the vocabulary. Less verbal prompting will need to take place.

Q. Does a child go through all five stages?

A. No. One child may skip stage 1 and master stages 2, 3 and 4 while another may not progress past stage 1. Each child's potential is different and affects their acquisition of verbal communication skills. That is why it is important to expose young children to a variety of communication techniques, both verbal and nonverbal. When we do this, we ensure that each child will become a "communicator," whether or not they develop speech.

Q. How long does it take to go through five stages of verbal play?

A. One child might move through stages 2 and 3 in a ten-minute verbal play session. Another may expand their skills over a period of months. Others may not move beyond the first stage.

Q. In stage 5, why is it necessary to verbally prompt by using a second adult for a child's response?

A. In stages 2 through 4, one adult can usually perform his own turn and perform as the prompter as needed. However, in stage 5, a second adult is invaluable as a prompter. If a second adult is not used while training conversational speech, the child may think that the prompt is part of the question since the same person is saying it. This may result in further confusion.

Q. Won't the child become confused anyway by the second adult's prompts?

A. There is an art to prompting. Before prompting, the second adult must wait long enough for the child to adequately process the information he has received. However, if he waits too long, the child may display signs of anxiety and choose to leave the situation. The waiting time to prompt an answer must continue to be longer and longer as the verbal play session progresses. This gives the child a chance to respond without the prompt. Also, the prompting must be done close to the child's ear and spoken in a whisper. It must appear very different from the conversational tone used by the first adult.

Q. Stage 3 entails "Single word on a topic." Do you mean that a topic can be built around a single word?

A. Yes. Some children have mastered joint action routines and display adequate staying power but possess limited emergent language. They do not yet speak in phrases or sentences but with single words. They are prime candidates for learning how to stay on a topic in this stage. Other children may have more language but not the staying power. So they may not respond to a longer routine being built around a phrase. These particular children respond best when a verbal routine is played at a much faster pace. This is possible with "Single word on a topic."

Q. How does the adult incorporate a cue and reinforcing turn into the third stage, "Single word on a topic'?

A. The cue might be a startled look or gasp after their single word is said. The reinforcer comes next and can be anything the child enjoys as long as it is quick. The fast pace of this exchange needs to remain intact. Then the adult waits expectantly for the child's next single word on the same topic.

OBJECTIVES WORKSHEET

Build verbal play routines throughout stages 1 to 5

CHILD'S NAME_____

CURRENT LEVEL

This child does not yet engage in a turn-taking routine where one partner's words are connected to the other's. His interactions lack "conversational flow." His words and phrases are isolated.

Date initiated_____ Date mastered_____

1. Given a verbal play stage 1 "Verbal and physical imitation, no topic" routine, the adult will imitate the child's movements and vocalizations and the child will keep the interaction going by varying the movements, sounds, single words and/or phrases.

Date initiated_____ Date mastered_____

2. Given a verbal play stage 2 "Single words and sounds, random topics" routine and the adult assigning meaning to the child's sounds, the child will toss single words and sounds back and forth with the adult for ten minutes.

Date initiated_____ Date mastered_____

3. Given a verbal play stage 3 "Single word on one topic" routine, the child will remain in one category as single words are passed back and forth.

Date initiated_____ Date mastered_____

4. Given a verbal play stage 4 "Phrases and sentences on one topic" routine, the child will remain in one category as phrases and sentences are passed back and forth.

Date initiated_____ Date mastered_____

5. Given a stage 5 "Prompted conversational speech on one familiar topic" routine and two adults, the child will hear a series of

questions/statements by the first adult and repeat the whispered answers, prompted by the second adult, to keep the "conversation" going.

Date initiated_____ Date mastered_____

6. Given a stage 5 "Prompted conversational speech on one familiar topic" routine and two adults, the child will hear a series of questions/statements by the first adult and respond with a novel unprompted answer, to keep the "conversation" going.

...find patience enough in yourself to endure, and simplicity enough to believe; that you may acquire more and more confidence in that which is difficult... And for the rest, let life happen to you. Believe me: life is right, in any case.

Rainer Maria Rilke, *Letters to a Young Poet*

DEVELOPING VERBAL PLAY THROUGH MOVEMENT AND TOUCH

KEY POINTS

Losing interest in you? Lost in his own repetitive phrases? Keep touching. Keep moving

> *During verbal play, incorporating movement and touch into the reinforcing turn will aid the child's staying power.*

> *Intermittent movement and touch can be used throughout the routine, becoming the glue that links the adult and child's turns together.*

> *Movement or touch must be exaggerated and sudden so that an element of surprise exists and startles the child.*

> *Movement and touch are crucial elements in developing verbal play stages 1 to 4. In stage 5 of verbal play, the prompted conversation is the reinforcer. A cue and reinforcing turn are no longer necessary. The "look" and "feel" of an actual conversation takes place and movement and touch are dropped.*

In stages 2, 3 and 4 of verbal play, movement and touch can be incorporated in several ways. When exaggerated, they can be implemented as the reinforcer after the child has successfully flipped a desired word from a category and inserted it into the verbal pattern. Or, movement and touch can be utilized intermittently throughout the routine as a vehicle for linking the separate words of the routine together.

Either way, when a *sudden* touch or movement is built into the routine, it will *startle* the child, which brings the focus back to the adult and the impending social connection. Movement and touch will help provide the staying power necessary to build the child's verbal skills in a playful context. Together, they can transform a series of verbal play turns into a memorable ten-minute patterned routine.

LET'S IMAGINE

How to develop verbal play patterns by using movement and touch with the verbal play format of Imitate–Select–Model–Prompt

EXAMPLE

Erik is on a tricycle and bumps into a slide. An adult sees the incident and hears the child exclaim a phrase afterwards: "Oh no, look out!'

PROBLEM

Erik is often observed slamming his body into large pieces of classroom equipment. His interactive play is rough. He is referred to as a "hectic" child. He requires a great deal of vestibular movement and heavy input into the joints to supply his system with sensory feedback. Since he is often "on the run," his staying power is weak.

SOLUTION

The adult attempts to develop a verbal pattern by imitating Erik and adding the noun at the end of his phrase. The noun is "flipped" through the toy classification. The adult knows that a verbal play game with Erik must involve heavy input into the joints and fast, jerky movements. Moving quickly in a linear vestibular motion and bumping into things will increase his staying power as well as provide sensory input. The adult observes him in this type of movement during free play and seizes the moment, making a verbal play game out of his actions and verbalization.

OH NO, LOOK OUT!

Child: Oh no, look out!

Adult: Oh no, look out <u>slide</u>! (*Imitate.*) (*Select.*)

Child: Oh my.

Adult: Oh my.

Child: *Pretends to cry.*

Adult: *Pretends to cry.*

Child: Crash! *Falls down, throwing feet into the air.*

Adult: Crash! *Falls down, throwing feet into the air. Adult continues to imitate verbally and physically while looking for an ending to the sequence and an opportunity to begin the sequence again by repeating the child's initial phrase.*

Child: *Laughs loudly.*

Adult: *Laughs loudly.*

Child: *Climbs back on tricycle. Adult sees this as an opportunity to begin the sequence again. In order to establish a verbal pattern the adult will now demonstrate how to change the last word but remain in the same classification by modeling new toy nouns three times.*

> In order to demonstrate a verbal pattern, the adult models how to continually change one word in a phrase while remaining in one category.

Adult: Oh no, look out <u>fort</u>. *Adult looks over at fort to visually cue the child. Adult waits expectantly to see if the child needs physical prompting to bump into the fort. The adult is attempting to set up the pattern that was played a few minutes earlier but with a new "toy" noun (first model).*

Child: Oh no, look out <u>fort</u>. *The child bumps the tricycle gently into the fort. He has responded to the modeling of the adult. He has also responded to the visual cue of the adult's eye gaze from the child to the fort. Physical prompting of the adult bumping the tricycle into the fort was not necessary. Since the child repeated this phrase, the verbal pattern is emerging.*

> The adult models the emerging pattern three different times before expecting the child to understand and participate.

Adult: Oh my. *The adult is temporarily saying the lines first and the child is now imitating. This is meant to cue the child to the idea that they are repeating the same sequence.*

Child: Oh my.

Adult: *Pretends to cry.*

Child: *Pretends to cry.*

Adult: Crash! *Falls down, throwing feet into the air.*

Child: Crash! *Falls down, throwing feet into the air.*

Adult: *Laughs loudly.*

Child: *Laughs loudly. Adult begins sequence again.*

Child: *Climbs back on tricycle.*

Adult: Oh no, look out <u>teeter totter</u>. (*second model*).

Child: Oh no, look out <u>teeter totter</u>.

Adult: Oh my.

Child: Oh my.

Adult: *Pretends to cry.*

Child: *Pretends to cry.*

Adult: Crash! *Falls down, throwing feet into the air.*

Child: Crash! *Falls down, throwing feet into the air.*

Adult: *Laughs loudly.*

Child: *Laughs loudly. Begin sequence again.*

Child: *Climbs back on tricycle.*

Adult: Oh no, look out <u>car</u> (*third model*).

Child: Oh no, look out <u>car</u>.

Adult: Oh my.

Child: Oh my.

Adult: *Pretends to cry.*

Child: *Pretends to cry.*

Adult: Crash! *Falls down, throwing feet into the air.*

Child: Crash! *Falls down, throwing feet into the air.*

Adult: *Laughs loudly.*

Child: *Laughs loudly. Begin sequence again.*

Adult: Oh no, look out <u>ball</u> …<u>wagon</u>… <u>doll</u>? (*Prompt.*)

Child: Oh no, look out <u>doll</u>.

Adult: Oh my.

Child: Oh my.

Adult: *Pretends to cry loudly* (*cue*).

Child: *Pretends to cry.*

When the child repeats one of the modeled or prompted words in a verbal game, he is demonstrating an understanding of the verbal pattern.

Increased volume of the cue lets the child know that the end of the sequence is near and the reinforcing turn is coming.

Adult: Crash! *Falls down dramatically, throwing feet wildly in air* (reinforcer).

Child: Crash! *Falls down dramatically, throwing feet wildly in air.*

Adult: *Laughs loudly.*

Child: *Laughs loudly.*

Repeat for ten minutes in which child and adult continue the sequence and substitute other toys in the phrase: ball, truck, and wagon.

WHAT? WHEN? WHY?

Answers to common questions

Q. How does movement aid vocalization?

A. If the movement is highly desirable, the child will be motivated to try harder. Perhaps he will perform at a higher verbal level to have the touch or movement repeated. Studies have also shown a connection between vestibular movement and expressive language. (Jensen, 1998)

Q. Why does the movement or touch need to be sudden?

A. It needs to startle the child. This builds excitement and keeps the child in close proximity, wanting more.

Q. In the "Crash" example, the child originally fell to the floor and said, "Crash." When you repeated the sequence the second time with a "flipped" word, *you* dropped to the floor and said "Crash" before he did. I thought that "Crash" was his turn in the sequence.

A. It was but I didn't want to take the chance of him not saying it again. I could see a pattern emerging so I modeled his original turn for him. This showed him that we were repeating a section of his previous play and vocalizations *together*. It doesn't matter whose turn it is as long as a predictable sequence emerges. Regardless of who takes what turn, it is the *sequence* that needs to be repeated exactly the same way each time.

OBJECTIVES WORKSHEET

Build verbal play routines through the aid of movement and touch

CHILD'S NAME_____

CURRENT LEVEL

This child may vocalize words but lack the staying power when engaged. His need for vestibular input and heavy pressure through touch may be high. Movement and touch continue to be strong reinforcers in verbal play games.

Date initiated_____ Date mastered_____

1. Given a verbal play/movement interaction that is suddenly stopped at the "flipped" word, the child will continue the routine by stating a novel, modeled, or prompted word, so that the movement will continue.

Date initiated_____ Date mastered_____

2. Given a verbal play/movement interaction with an adult, the child will remain engaged for ten minutes.

In our willingness to step into the unknown, the field of all possibilities, we surrender ourselves to the creative mind that orchestrates the dance of the universe.

Deepak Chopra, *The Seven Spiritual Laws for Parents*

DEVELOPING VERBAL PLAY THROUGH RHYTHM AND RHYME

KEY POINTS

How can I pick one of his words to flip through a category when his speech is so limited? Use his favorite song

Chant rhymes or sing songs that are favored by the child.

Select one phrase of the song. "Flip" one word of the phrase.

Model the phrase three times with a new "flipped" word each time, hesitate at the flipped word and look expectantly at the child.

If the child doesn't volunteer a word from the chosen category, verbally prompt three words with a questioning intonation.

Songs and rhymes lend themselves well to the development of verbal play patterns. Consider using the child's favored songs or rhymes from previous giggle time routines. The verbal play format of Imitate–Select–Model–Prompt is followed with the exception of imitation. Imitation is not necessary since the adult begins the routine with a song instead of imitating one of the child's phrases. The adult begins by singing or chanting a portion of a rhyme, accompanied by motion. The adult *selects* one phrase of the song and experiments with "flipping" one noun or adjective. This part of the song is sung three times and each time this chosen phrase is sung, the adult *models* how to flip one word through a category. Thus, the child is hearing one phrase sung with three different words from a category.

After the adult models three times, she verbally *prompts* three words in a row from the category. By doing so with a questioning inflection, she demonstrates an expectation of the child to repeat one of the prompted words. Modeling and prompting continues until the child catches on to the pattern and fills in a word from the category on his turn. When this happens, the child displays an understanding of the emerging pattern and the adult's modeling and prompting are no longer necessary. It is, however, time to add the *cue* and *reinforcing turn* to the verbal play routine that has just developed. The verbal play routine is then played repetitively for ten minutes.

Caution. Do not attempt to build a verbal play turn taking around an entire song or rhyme. Two, or at the most three, lines of a song or rhyme are sufficient for building a verbal play routine. If more lines are sung, staying power might be lost since the time elapsed between the flipped words might be too long and the pattern may be forgotten.

> *Do not sing an entire rhyme. Two or three phrases can be broken down into the entire turn taking.*

> *As the child's skills develop, it is possible to "flip" more than one word in a phrase.*

As a child's skill in remaining on a topic and auditory memory improve, it is possible to flip more than one word in a phrase of a song. "Down on <u>Grampa's</u> farm there was a little <u>yellow</u> <u>duck</u>" can be changed to "<u>Down on Daddy's</u> farm there was a little <u>orange</u> <u>horse</u>." This can occur if your memory can match the child's and withstand the challenge!

LET'S IMAGINE

How to use a song or rhyme to encourage verbal play

EXAMPLE

In the following example, the child is sitting face to face on the adult's lap. The adult begins reciting the beginning of the "Farmer Rides" rhyme, listed as "This is the Way the Ladies Ride" in Chapter 2. Since the adult begins a rhyme, the first step of the verbal play format, *Imitation* (of the child's spontaneous language), is not necessary. The adult begins with the remaining components of the format, Select–Model–Prompt, as a verbal play routine develops.

PROBLEM

Lindsay's expressive vocalizations are limited upon demand. When expected to vocalize, she often lowers her head. Her staying power is less when her turns are expected to be verbal as well as nonverbal.

SOLUTION

The verbal play format, which offers adult modeling and prompting, will take the pressure off her to retrieve words on her own. The adult chooses the "Farmer Rides" rhyme around which to build a verbal play routine since it is a favorite rhyme of the child's. The adult selects one word of the first phrase to "flip." Since Lindsay is familiar receptively with farm animal names, the adult changes the word "farmer" to "cow" and then proceeds to model and prompt her through the "flipping" of the farm animal category. Lindsay is also moved up and down on the adult's lap to the beat of the rhyme for additional vestibular input. This also gives the adult the opportunity to hold the child's hands as she is bounced, further ensuring that her staying power will increase.

FARMER RIDES

Adult: This is the way the <u>cow</u> rides, the <u>cow</u> rides, and the <u>cow</u> rides. *Bounces child on knees, holding hands (select).*

Child: *Eye contact.*

Adult: This...is...the...way...the...<u>cow</u>...rides...

Child: *Social smile.*

Adult: Moo-moo-moo-moo-moo. *Throws head down and quickly says phrase while tickling.*

Child: *Laughs.*

Adult: *Laughs.*

Adult: This is the way the <u>chicken</u> rides, the <u>chicken</u> rides, and the <u>chicken</u> rides. *Bounces child on knees, holding hands (first model).*

Child: *Eye contact.*

Adult: This...is...the...way...the...<u>chicken</u>...rides...

Child: *Social smile.*

Adult: Cluck-cluck-cluck-cluck-cluck. *Throws head down and quickly says phrase while tickling.*

Child: *Laughs.*

> An initial objective of verbal play would be for the child to state a word from the category that has been previously modeled or prompted by the adult.

Adult: *Laughs.* This is the way the <u>sheep</u> rides, the <u>sheep</u> rides, and the <u>sheep</u> rides. *Bounces child on knees, holding hands (second model).*

Child: *Eye contact.*

Adult: This…is…the…way…the…<u>sheep</u>…rides…

Child: *Social smile.*

Adult: Baa-baa-baa-baa-baa-baa. *Throws head down and quickly says phrase while tickling.*

Child: *Laughs.*

Adult: *Laughs.* This is the way the <u>horse</u> rides, the <u>horse</u> rides, and the <u>horse</u> rides. *Bounces child on knees, holding hands (third model).*

> The stating of novel words from the category, not modeled or prompted, is a higher-level skill but a desirable long-term objective.

Child: *Eye contact.*

Adult: This…is…the…way…the…<u>horse</u>…rides.

Child: *Social smile.*

Adult: Neigh-neigh-neigh-neigh-neigh. *Throws head down and quickly says phrase while tickling.*

> The adult should model the categorical "flipping" of a word three times before expecting the child to choose one.

Child: *Laughs.*

Adult: *Laughs and then begins the sequence again, this time verbally prompting three animals in a row with a questioning intonation. The adult waits expectantly for the child to fill in one of the farm animal names after prompting. The goal is for the child to continue the pattern on her turn. Eventually, she will insert a name each time the adult stops at the "flipped" word in the phrase and looks expectantly. An initial objective would be to retrieve farm animals that the adult has modeled or prompted. Word retrieval of novel farm animals not mentioned before is a higher-level skill.*

> After the verbal game is firmly established and repetitively played, the child will begin to insert a modeled, prompted or novel word from the category each time the adult stops at the "flipped" word in the phrase and looks expectantly.

Adult: This is the way the <u>goat</u>…<u>pig</u>…<u>duck</u>? *Hesitates and waits expectantly (verbal).*

Child: Duck! *Child chooses one of the prompted words, understanding the pattern. Now adult begins refining the cue and reinforcing turn. The "core" of the routine is next and is the portion that will be repetitively played.*

Adult: This is the way the <u>duck</u> rides, the <u>duck</u> rides, and the <u>duck</u> rides. *Bounces child on knees, holding hands.*

Child: *Eye contact.*

Adult: This...is...the...way...the...<u>duck</u>...rides... *Throws head back dramatically (cue).*

Child: *Social smile.*

Adult: Quack, quack, quack, quack, quack. *Throws head down and quickly says phrase while tickling (reinforcer).*

Child: *Laughs.*

Adult: *Laughs.*

Repeat sequence for ten minutes, with various farm animals.

WHAT? WHEN? WHY?

Answers to common questions

Q. Why do songs and rhymes lend themselves to the development of verbal play patterns?

A. There are many reasons why they are helpful tools for building verbal play skills. Each rhyme or song contains a beat. The beat can be accented through movement and emphasized with your voice. The familiarity of the rhyme or song also provides immediate interest, ensuring staying power. It is a short cut to the development of a verbal play routine if the child does not supply an array of vocalizations from which to imitate and select a phrase. When one or two phrases are chosen from a song or rhyme, the majority of the routine is near completion. Two more turns from the child turns it into a four-turn routine. Also, since the tune or rhyme is familiar to both partners, it is easily remembered from day to day. This is helpful when the adult may have ten routines to remember and spontaneously retrieve with each child!

Even though I strongly encourage the adult to write all routines down, sometimes notes are not handy. In this case, it is very easy to move into a verbal play routine based upon a familiar song and rhyme.

Q. How do you know which phrases to pick from the rhyme or song?

A. Use the beginning line and break it into two adult turns, especially if the child's staying power is weak. The first few lines are chosen because the beginning of a favored song or rhyme is most familiar to a child and will bring a smile of recognition to his face. The second line can incorporate the cue and the reinforcing turn.

Q. What do you mean by rhymes?

A. Familiar nursery rhymes and finger plays are useful rhymes as well as picture books that have repetitive text. Choose one or two lines from the text and build a patterned verbal play routine around it.

Q. Can you give me additional verbal play examples demonstrating how to choose a categorical word to "flip" from rhymes and songs?

A. The word "spider" in the "Eensy Weensy Spider" song could be "flipped" through the bug category: ant, bee, butterfly, grasshopper, and so on. The word "Thumbkin" in the "Where is Thumbkin" song could be "flipped" to any body part: nose, leg, foot, hand, mouth, and so on. The word "boat" in the "Row, Row, Row the Boat" song could be "flipped" to any mode of transportation: plane, truck, car, fire engine, and so on. Remember, it doesn't have to make sense. It's verbal *play*. The key to using a particular rhyme or song is knowing that the child is familiar with the chosen topic of the "flipped" category. If he is not, it is imperative to supply him with visual cues to support his word retrieval.

Q. It seems so easy when you do it, but how do you turn a song or rhyme into a routine? How much of it should I use? What parts are my turns and what parts are the child's?

A. After you have modeled and prompted words in a category for the child, he will eventually begin "flipping" the category with you. This demonstrates his understanding of the emergent pattern. Once the child demonstrates this understanding, the adult can stop abruptly each time before the "flipped" word and wait for the child's response. The child's turn will be the "flipped" word. The next part of the verbal play routine incorporates a cue. The adult states the next phrase of the rhyme and cues it. The child proceeds with a nonverbal turn and the adult ends the routine with a reinforcing turn. This sequence is then repeated for ten minutes. Note the following examples in the next question/answer.

Q. What are some examples of verbal routines, involving rhymes that have been completed by an adult and child?

A. See below.

EENSY WEENSY SPIDER (CATEGORY OF BUGS)

Adult: Eensy Weensy _____ (*Selected phrase.*)

Child: <u>lady bug</u> (*flipped word*).

Adult: w…e…n…t *said slowly with rising inflection* (*cue*).

Child: *Social smile.*

Adult: up the water spout! *Twirls child in spinning chair* (*reinforcer*).

Verbal routine is played for ten minutes with child inserting various bugs into the phrase on his turn.

WHERE IS THUMBKIN (CATEGORY OF BODY PARTS)

Adult: Where is _____ (*Selected phrase.*)

Child: <u>ear</u> (*flipped word*).

Adult: How are you today, s…i…r? (*Cue.*)

Child: *Eye contact.*

Adult: Run away! Run away! *Flips child backwards off lap twice* (*reinforcer*).

Verbal routine is played for ten minutes with child inserting various body parts into the phrase.

ROW, ROW, ROW THE BOAT (CATEGORY OF TRANSPORTATION)

Adult: Row, row, row the _____ (*Selected phrase.*)

Child: <u>car</u> (*flipped word*).

Adult: Gently down the (*whispers*) (*cue*).

Child: *Eye contact.*

Adult: Stream! *Pulls child on blanket three feet* (*reinforcer*).

Verbal routine is played for ten minutes with child inserting various modes of transportation into the phrase.

OBJECTIVES WORKSHEET

Build verbal play routines around familiar rhymes and aid the skill of staying on a topic

CHILD'S NAME_____

CURRENT LEVEL

This child enjoys verbal and physical imitation but needs practice staying on a topic. He is either in verbal play stage 2 (Single words and sounds, random topics,) verbal play stage 3 (Single words on one topic) or verbal play stage 4 (Phrases and sentences on one topic).

Date initiated_____ Date mastered_____

1. Given a phrase of a song/rhyme that is stopped at a "flipped" word, the child will maintain the verbal interaction by retrieving a word that he has heard the adult *model* on one of their turns in this session. (Adult may have modeled that particular word in this turn-taking session and the child retrieves it and uses it on his turn.)

Date initiated_____ Date mastered_____

2. Given a phrase of a song/rhyme that is stopped at a "flipped" word, the child will maintain the verbal interaction by stating one of the *prompted* words in the classification. (Adult has modeled the pattern three different times and now comes to the "flipped" word and verbally prompts three words in a row in the classification. The child chooses to say one of those words on his turn, displaying an emerging understanding of a verbal play pattern.)

Date initiated_____ Date mastered_____

3. Given a phrase of a song/rhyme that is stopped at a "flipped" word, the child will maintain the verbal interaction by generating a *new word* in the same classification. (Child retrieves a word to "flip" in the category that has not yet been mentioned in this session. Adult may have used that particular word when previously engaged in this verbal game on a different day, but the child retrieves it in a later verbal play setting. It might also be a novel word from the category that has not yet been stated.)

Play with words back and forth; words are your child's most important toys.

James MacDonald, *Becoming Partners with Children*

DEVELOPING VERBAL PLAY THROUGH VISUAL CUES

KEY POINTS

Word retrieval a problem? Use visual cues as props

Object or picture cues can aid word retrieval during verbal play.

If a child has difficulty retrieving words from memory in verbal play, object props are useful tools. When set near the verbal play area, they can trigger the child's use of nouns in a particular classification. For example, plastic foods, animals, or articles of clothing might be placed in view depending on the verbal play pattern.

However, be prepared to incorporate the prop into the joint action routine if necessary. Having the visual cues of the nouns nearby may be a distraction and the child's primary focus may shift from you to a prop. The prop should be kept within the child's visual field and within your grasp. If it is within the child's grasp, he will manipulate the prop excessively and attention to the developing verbal game will be lost.

Keep control of the manipulation of props.

Incorporate the object prop into your reinforcing turn.

One way to minimally expose the child to the visual cue is to pick it up and use it in the reinforcing turn for added interest. It can be tossed in the air, nuzzled into the child's neck, or moved to the rhythm of the cue. The prop can then be temporarily placed out of view. This encourages the child to gaze at the assorted visual cues once again on his next turn and retrieve a different noun for the verbal pattern.

Despite the above precautions, tangible props may prove to be too distracting for a particular child. If this is the case, photos of objects may be helpful. However, the child must have an understanding that pictures represent objects before they can be utilized as an aid in

Photos, "themed" pictorial clothing, and picture books can aid verbal play if objects distract the child.

word retrieval. In addition to photos, I have worn sweatshirts and smocks depicting various themes. A "farm" sweatshirt proved to be an invaluable tool for eliciting animal names in a verbal pattern. Children have also worn clothing that has been used as visual cues. One student wore a shirt depicting various modes of transportation and it became the visual cue for two fellow students. Birthday accessories such as tablecloths, party hats and birthday plates have also proved helpful since they are themed in one category as well. Verbal play might also be constructed around a favorite picture book. One line of the book can be repeated and the "flipped" word can be themed by pointing to the accompanying pictures on the child's turn.

Choose props from a category that the child is interested in.

Your imagination, combined with the visual tools in your environment, can lessen a child's struggle with verbal play. Allow your creativity and the interests of the child to guide you.

LET'S IMAGINE

How to incorporate visual tools into a verbal play routine to aid the child's language retrieval

EXAMPLE

Plastic animals are on a table. Adult and child are in chairs, facing each other, next to the table. The props are in one classification area, "farm animals."

PROBLEM

Vince has difficulty retrieving words during verbal play games. He enjoys playing with language but some of his turns are still nonverbal. He is still in need of movement, a cue, and a reinforcing turn for staying power.

SOLUTION

Vince is familiar with farm animal names through the use of various musical videos about farms, thematic hands-on instruction of a farm unit and through the repetition of farm songs. Visual cues of plastic farm animals are within visual range but not close enough for him to touch. Incorporate an element of surprise and movement to aid staying power. When the adult is in doubt as to what to say or do next as the routine develops, she imitates!

OLD MACDONALD HAD A FARM

Child: <u>Pig</u>, <u>pig</u>, come back! *Looks over at pig on table.*

Adult: *Picks up pig and hides it under child's shirt, saying* Oink, oink, oink!

Child: *Lifts shirt, pig drops out.* Oh my gosh!

Adult: Oh my gosh! *Quickly holds child's hands and pulls him toward her in a quick frontal movement (imitate).*

Child: *Pretends to cry.*

Adult: *Pretends to cry. Holds on to child's waist and moves child in sagittal side-to-side movement while crying. Adult adds action to crying imitation.*

Child: Good night! *Lays head down on adult's lap.*

Adult: Good night! *Lays head down next to child and snores.*

Child: *Snores (imitates).*

Adult: Wake up!

Child: Wake up! *(Imitates.)*

Adult: <u>Chicken</u>, <u>chicken,</u> come back! *(Select.) (First model.)*

Child: <u>Chicken</u>, <u>chicken</u>, come back! *Child verbally imitates, following the verbal pattern.*

Adult: *Continues the sequence above as she picks up the chicken and hides it under child's shirt.* Cluck, cluck, cluck.

Child: *Lifts shirt, chicken drops out.* Oh my gosh!

Adult: Oh my gosh! *Quickly lifts child's hands and pulls him toward her in a quick frontal movement, once again adding action to verbal imitation for increased interest.*

Child: *Pretends to cry.*

Adult: *Pretends to cry. Holds on to child's waist and moves child in sagittal side-to-side movement while crying. Adult adds action to crying imitation.*

> The adult can visually cue the child by looking over at the props as a new noun is spoken.

> When the adult looks over at the props it cues the child that the props are important. The child's gaze may follow the adult's in joint attention. If it doesn't, the adult can briefly manipulate the object as she states the prop's name.

Child: Good night! *Lays head down on adult's lap.*

Adult: Good night! *Lays head down next to child and snores.*

Child: *Snores, imitates.*

Adult: Wake up!

Child: Wake up! (*Imitates.*)

Adult: *Adult continues repeating the above sequence two more times, incorporating two more models.* Sheep, sheep, come back (*second model*). Cow, cow, come back (*third model*).

Adult: Turkey…duck…horse? *Adult glances over at animal props as these words are stated* (*prompt*).

Child: Horse!

Adult: Horse, horse, come back.

Child: Horse, horse, come back.

Adult: *Picks up horse and hides it under child's shirt, while saying,* Neigh, neigh, neigh!

Child: *Lifts shirt, horse drops out.* Oh my gosh!

Adult: Oh my gosh! *Quickly moves child's hands and pulls him toward her in a quick frontal movement* (*cue*).

Child: *Pretends to cry.*

Adult: *Pretends to cry. Holds on to child's waist and moves child in a sagittal side-to-side movement while crying* (*reinforcer*).

Child: Good night! *Lays head down on adult's lap.*

Adult: Good night! *Lays head down next to child and snores.*

Child: *Snores.*

Adult: Wake up!

Child: Wake up!

Game continues with other farm animals within view on the table for ten minutes.

Old Macdonald

To aid word retrieval in verbal play, place props from a familiar category nearby.

Verbal play on a topic is interspersed with verbal imitation. An action added to verbal imitation will increase interest and encourage staying power.

WHAT? WHEN? WHY?

Answers to common questions

Q. How can props be incorporated into a verbal pattern?

A. Props depicting different nouns of the same category are displayed nearby or depicted on an article of clothing that one of you is wearing. They are within a few feet of the child. As the adult models and prompts the child in the category, he looks in the direction of the props and points toward them. The child may use language, eye gaze, or gesture toward the prop to indicate their choice as to which word to incorporate into the phrase.

Q. At what point in the verbal play routine do you introduce props?

A. After you have followed the verbal play format of Imitate–Select–Model–Prompt and the child is still not inserting a modeled or prompted word when you hesitate and look expectantly, it may be time to introduce props. By placing the actual picture or object of the nouns that you are mentioning nearby, you are offering the child the visual cues of the words you are modeling and prompting. This may aid understanding and trigger the child's verbalization in that category.

Q. How can verbal play be built around a book?

A. Pick the child's favorite book. As you read it with the child, pick out *one* catchy phrase. State the phrase with animation, cue one word of the phrase, wait expectantly for the child's turn, and then complete the phrase with a reinforcing turn. Begin the phrase again, this time choosing one word in the phrase that can be flipped through a category. As you begin the modeling portion of the verbal play format, look at the illustrations on the page and use this visual cue to model three words for the flipped word. After a few more minutes verbally prompt the flipped word for the child with a questioning tone, and *wait*. The child will probably state one of the modeled or prompted words that he can see in the illustrations of the book. Continue with the cue and reinforcer to build the verbal routine and then begin again.

Q. You said, "If the child shifts his interest to the prop, incorporate it into the joint action routine." How do I do that?

A. Add it to your reinforcing turn by hiding it in his clothing, tossing it in the air, moving it to the rhythm of the cue or nuzzling him with it.

Q. What if you retrieve the visual cue prop from the child, incorporate it into the reinforcing turn, place it out of view, and the child wants it back?

A. First, try not to give the child an opportunity to demonstrate that he wants it back. If this occurs, you are waiting too long before beginning the developed sequence of turns again. *Quickly* move back into the verbal play sequence, being sure that your initial turn is exaggerated and animated to pull the attention back to you. Once again become the toy and his interest will shift back to you. If it does not, it's important to follow his lead. You can do this by *altering* the verbal play sequence slightly, letting it revolve around the prop he is attracted to. For example, if the category was "farm animals" and the visual cue prop was a plastic "pig," you might alter the verbal game by only using the noun that the child is interested in, "pig," but place a different adjective before it that can be flipped. Various colors, numbers, emotions, and so on could be the word before "pig" that is flipped. Red pig, green pig, yellow pig, or one pig, three pigs, eight pigs, or sad pig, mad pig, and so on might become the new category that is "flipped." Altering should be attempted before you give up the sequence that has been developed and create a totally new one.

OBJECTIVES WORKSHEET

Aid verbal play by providing visual cues during the interaction

CHILD'S NAME_____

CURRENT LEVEL

This child successfully engages in reciprocal interactions for ten minutes and receptively understands many categories of words. However, word retrieval is difficult and visual cueing is necessary for success. His staying power weakens when he is asked to retrieve a word in a category on his turn. Incorporating movement into one of the verbal play turns will aid staying power until the verbal play becomes stronger.

Date initiated_____ Date mastered_____

1. Given verbal play with visual cues, movement and a one-foot conversational play space, the child will remain engaged with the adult for five minutes.

Date initiated_____ Date mastered_____

2. Given verbal play with visual cues, movement and a one-foot conversational play space, the child will remain engaged with the adult for ten minutes.

Date initiated_____ Date mastered_____

3. Given verbal play with visual cues in which the adult models, prompts and then hesitates before the "flipped" word, the child will gaze at the props and state one of those words, inserting it into the pattern to maintain interaction.

One of the hardest lessons we have to learn in this life...is to see the divine, the celestial, the pure in the common, the near at hand...to see that heaven lies about us here in this world.

John Burroughs, *Angels on Earth*

DEVELOPING VERBAL PLAY WITHOUT MOVEMENT, RHYTHM AND RHYME, OR VISUAL CUES

KEY POINTS

Will he ever be able to spontaneously play with language?

Spontaneous verbal play without visual cues, rhyme, song or movement is the goal.
Any phrase that the child utters can be used in verbal play.
Through verbal play, the child learns that sharing words back and forth can be fun and rewarding.

Once you have experienced an array of verbal routines with visual cues, movement, and rhymes, it is time to try some without. Our goal, of course, is to reach a point where verbal play can occur naturally and at any time. Any passing animal, mode of transportation, sneeze or phrase can easily be transformed into playful verbiage. One simply takes a child's uttered phrase and begins the verbal play format. Whether you are in a store, on the playground, in a restaurant or on a walk, playing with language in a relaxed way can be a vehicle for further development of the social connection.

LET'S IMAGINE

How to develop verbal play patterns by seizing the moment without using rhyme, props, or movement

EXAMPLE

In the following example, both child and adult are watching the school bus pull away. The child initiates the phrase "Bye bus."

PROBLEM

Lisa interacts in a variety of verbal play routines, easily "flipping" words through categories. However, all of her verbal play games incorporate movement, visual cues and chants or rhymes. She does not yet spontaneously play with language in a relaxed way without the need for movement, cues, and rhymes from the adult. She is in stage 4 of verbal play: Phrases and sentences on one topic. The use of a cue and reinforcing turn are still optional and depend upon her staying power.

SOLUTION

The adult seizes the opportunity to develop a verbal patterned sequence when the adult and child are getting off the bus. As this is an everyday occurrence and is not "set up," the adult attempts to move the child toward engaging in verbal play anywhere and at any time. The adult begins the verbal play pattern by changing the noun at the end of the child's spontaneous phrase. The adult develops a pattern, using various modes of transportation, by keeping the word "Bye" and changing the word "bus."

 BYE-BYE

> Child: Bye bus.
>
> Adult: Bye <u>bus</u> (*imitate*), (*select*). *Adds motion of waving hand.*
>
> Child: Come back later.
>
> Adult: Come back later. *Imitates and adds hands beside mouth in shouting posture.* Bye <u>car</u>. *Waves (first model).*
>
> Child: Bye <u>bus</u>.
>
> Adult: Come back later. *Adds hands beside mouth again.*
>
> Child: Come back later.
>
> Adult: Bye <u>ambulance</u>. *Waves (second model).*
>
> Child: Bye <u>bus</u>.
>
> Adult: Come back later. *Adds hands beside mouth again in shouting position.*
>
> Child: Come back later.
>
> Adult: Bye <u>truck</u>. *Waves (third model).*
>
> Child: Bye <u>bus</u>.

Attempt to engage the child in verbal play by seizing the moment throughout the day.

Drop the movement, props and rhyme but continue to use the verbal play format of Imitate-Select-Model-Prompt.

Adult: Come back later. *Adds hands beside mouth again in shouting position.*

Child: Come back later.

Adult: *Attempts transportation pattern again, prompting the changing of the noun through different modes of transportation.* Bye <u>train</u>...<u>helicopter</u>...<u>fire engine</u>? (*Prompt.*)

Child: Bye <u>fire engine</u>.

Adult: *Imitates and adds wave.* Bye <u>fire engine</u>.

Child: Come back later.

Adult: *Imitates and adds hands beside mouth.* Come back later.

He's got it! He now "flips" the noun in the category, moving through various modes of transportation. Sequence continues with boat, helicopter, airplane, police car, train, and so on. A cue and subtle reinforcing turn may not be needed in stage 4; however, they may be added if necessary for staying power.

WHAT? WHEN? WHY?

Answers to common questions

Q. Why did you pair the motion of a waving hand to "Bye bus" and the shouting posture of your hands beside your mouth to "Come back later'?

A. The motions become a visual cue when the adult begins to drop words of the pattern sequence. After the sequence has been played through several times, the adult drops the verbal cueing but continues the motion with animation. When the child sees the motion, he is more apt to retrieve and verbalize the phrase that was previously paired with it.

Q. What cue and reinforcing turn do you add when the child has moved beyond the need for visual props, rhymes and movement in developing verbal play?

A. You probably won't need a cue and reinforcing turn any longer. The child has now moved beyond the need for these tools and is closer to developing conversational speech. Your obvious enjoyment, smiles and laughter are now the reinforcers for the child as well as the warm connection between the two of you. If need be, exaggerate your facial expressions periodically throughout the verbal play for added interest. This will increase his attention and interest in you.

OBJECTIVES WORKSHEET

Build verbal play routines from the child's spontaneous language without movement, rhyme, cues, or reinforcing turn

CHILD'S NAME_____

CURRENT LEVEL

This child loves verbal play and easily follows the adult as she engages in the verbal play format of Imitate–Select–Model–Prompt. He "flips" through a category easily with an adult, "flipping" modeled, prompted and novel words with ease. He loves the playful exchange of words and no longer tends to need the cued turn of the adult or a reinforcing turn at the end of the verbal play pattern to sustain engagement. He is in stage 4 of verbal play: Phrases and sentences on one topic. He now needs spontaneous verbal play practice in various settings to further develop his vocabulary and ability to play with language. He is learning that language is spontaneously exchanged between people and is a social connection that brings great joy.

Date initiated_____ Date mastered_____

1. Given a spontaneous phrase spoken by the child and the adult modeling and prompting the category embedded in his phrase, the child will state one of the *modeled* or *prompted* words to maintain the interaction. (Classification categories might include colors, numbers, alphabet, clothing, body parts, farm animals, zoo animals, people's names, transportation, and food. Cue, reinforcing turn and movement are not necessary. Play with words is the reinforcer and is enough to sustain staying power.)

Date initiated_____ Date mastered_____

2. Given a spontaneous phrase spoken by the child and the adult modeling and prompting the category embedded in his phrase, the child will engage in verbal play and state a *novel* word to maintain the interaction. (Cue, reinforcing turn and movement are not necessary. Play with words is the reinforcer and is enough to sustain staying power. A novel word is one that has not been modeled or prompted by the adult in the ten-minute time period. The child may have heard it modeled or prompted at another time or thought of a new word in the category.)

Epilogue

Dear Jacob,

I was driving one morning when I became acutely aware of the surrounding black clouds. As I stopped momentarily, my eye was caught by the stark whiteness of a roof against the darkened sky. I stared without ceasing, attempting to etch its unusual beauty into my memory. Suddenly, the roof lifted and exploded into hundreds of gulls and doves in majestic flight. I gasped as they danced in a shimmer of white, floating together as one. I glanced again at the roof and smiled in amazement, now finding it as dark and gray as the surrounding sky. I quickly looked to others in nearby cars, hoping to share my awe. Their faces were still, their eyes dull, their attention elsewhere.

Sometimes we look and don't really see. Things are not always as they appear. Treasure can be hidden in the midst of darkness. If one perseveres, the darkness lifts and unseen gifts appear. They shine with great intensity in contrast to the former dismal backdrop.

My thoughts shifted to you, Jacob, and the parallel of this sight. You also appear to have a roof, a roof of limitations that make social contact and communication difficult. However, giggle time presented you with a "roof that lifted" and opened to new communicative behaviors and social responses. You too were more than what you appeared to be: a boy who appeared hard to reach but in reality shined with great intensity against the dark backdrop of isolation.

I will not be disappointed by the lack of enthusiasm of others as I witness small increments of your growth. All steps, no matter how small, are glorious and deserve applause. Just as the neighboring cars failed to see, my vision of you remains. My reference is derived from a different perspective.

It's time for you to move on, but your gifts continue. In the midst of future struggle I know I will find perseverance and endurance manifesting within me. They will beckon me around the dark crevices of self-doubt. As I rise to a new challenge, I will think of you: a dark-haired little boy with a smile that captured my heart. You have taught me to have insurmountable faith in the unseen and given witness to the idea that "A heart that has learned to trust can be at rest in the world" (Deepak Chopra, *The Path to Love*, Random House).

Love,

Miss Sue

Appendix

GIGGLE GAME WORKSHEET

Each giggle game developed between an adult and child is written on the worksheet cited below. These sheets are kept in a divided notebook separated by each student's name for easy reference. In addition to refreshing memory, recording dates played and adding alterations to games, these worksheets can be easily duplicated for home or school use to aid generalization.

Child_____Partner_____

Dates played_____

Game title_____

Cue _____

Reinforcing turn _____

Child's turn _____

Adult's turn _____

Child's turn _____

Adult's turn _____

Child's turn _____

Adult's turn _____

Child's turn _____

Adult's turn _____

Child's turn _____

Adult's turn _____

Child's turn _____

Adult's turn _____

Notes:

Bibliography

Books

Fey, M. (ed) (1986) *Language Intervention with Young Children.* San Diego: College-Hill Press.

Greenspan, S. (ed) (1998) *The Growth of the Mind.* Reading, MA: Addison-Wesley Publishing Co.

Janert, S. (ed) (2000) *Reaching the Young Autistic Child.* London: Free Association Books.

Jensen, E. (1998) *Teaching with the Brain in Mind.* Alexandria, VA: Association for Supervision and Curriculum Development.

Kranowitz, Carol Stock. (1998) *The Out of Sync Child.* New York: The Berkley Publishing Company.

MacDonald, J. (ed) (1989) *Becoming Partners with Children.* Ohio State University: Riverside Publishing Co.

Martin, E. (ed) (1988) *Baby Games.* Philadelphia, PA: Running Press.

Schuler, A. and Prizant, B. (1987) 'Facilitating Communication: Pre-Language Approaches.' In D. Cohen and A. Donnellan (eds) *Handbook of Autism and Pervasive Developmental Disorders.* New York: Wiley.

Articles

Gunsberg, A. (1989) 'Empowering Young Abused and Neglected Children through Contingency Play.' *Childhood Education,* Fall, 8–10.

MacDonald, J. (1998) *Communicating Partners: A Newsletter and Developmental Guide for Professionals and Parents of Children Developing Language.* Family Child Learning Center, 143 Northwest Ave., Building A, Tallmadge, Ohio 44278 (Fall).

Prizant, B. (1983) 'Echolalia in Autism: Assessment and Intervention.' *Seminars in Speech and Language 4,* 1.

Prizant, B. (1984) 'Assessment and Intervention Communicative Problems in Children with Autism.' *Communicative Disorders 9,* 9.

Tiegerman, E. and Primavera, L. (1981) 'Object Manipulation: An Interactional Strategy with Autistic Children.' *Journal of Autism and Developmental Disorders 11,* 4.

Young, J. (1988) 'Developing Social Conversation Skills: An Intervention Study of Preverbal Handicapped Children with their Parents.' Unpublished master's thesis, Ohio State University.